DUBLIN ZOO

An Illustrated History

Bornean orangutan Sibu.

DUBLIN ZOO

An Illustrated History

New edition

CATHERINE DE COURCY

Mabel Wray Press for

Published in 2019 by Mabel Wray Press for
Dublin Zoo

ISBN: 978-1-9997266-0-7

Book design and typesetting by Anú Design, Tara (www.anu-design.ie)
Book cover design by Wilson Creative (www.wilsoncreative.ie)
Typeset in Minion
Printed in Italy by Printer Trento

FSC
www.fsc.org

MIX
Paper from
responsible sources
FSC® C015829

Main Lake

Contents

Foreword

The long history of Dublin Zoo was put on record in 2009 for the first time with the publication of *Dublin Zoo: an illustrated history*. What emerged was that from the day it opened in 1831, Dublin Zoo had at its heart a mission to cultivate respect for wildlife and promote appreciation for every animal. And each successive generation has delivered on this mission according to the standards of the day.

For Philip Crampton, founder of the Zoo, the intention was to bring visitors close to animals in the hope that they would refrain from cruelty to animals generally. Until the mid-twentieth century, these close encounters included elephant rides, shaking hands with primates and handling young lions. During this time the keepers developed their skills and knowledge with little outside help. Their ability to care for exotic animals was evident in the international reputation Dublin Zoo developed for breeding lions. Their rapport with the animals was also evident in the number of animals that intermingled with visitors. The keepers passed their skills and knowledge through the generations and, by the late twentieth century when a different approach was needed, the solid foundations for creating a new way of keeping animals was in place.

By now the world's zoos were taking on a vital role in the conservation of animals and promoting awareness about the serious threats to wildlife and biodiversity. Thankfully Dublin Zoo was extraordinarily fortunate with the very generous support given by successive Irish governments, beginning with the first of several substantial capital grants in 1994 and the valuable transfer of land from Áras an Uachtaráin in 1997. The challenge for the Zoo team was to establish an environment in which the animals could live in a natural way while keeping adventure, awe and inspiration as part of a memorable day out for visitors.

In 2005 a master plan was created to transform Dublin Zoo into an immersive wildlife experience with a very strong conservation message. Since then world-class habitats, each inspired by the wild, have been created including the Kaziranga Forest Trail, the African Savanna, the Gorilla Rainforest, the Sea Lion Cove and the Orangutan Forest. The habitats allow the animals to behave in much the same way as they would in the wild, breeding and raising their young. The design approach is extended to the entire Zoo so that all visitors are immersed in an experience of discovery and inspiration, which motivates us all to think about the natural world.

Dublin Zoo is a charity that is run by a voluntary council, which has been overseeing the running of the Zoo since 1831. The history shows us how it kept the Zoo going through very difficult times. Today with increased visitor numbers we generate a surplus, which is reinvested to further develop innovative habitats and visitor facilities. The changes of the past 25 years have transformed Dublin Zoo into a leading centre for conservation and learning, providing visitor experiences that inspire curiosity of the natural world. A large percentage of our visitors are children and each time they visit the Zoo, they learn something about the importance of protecting and nurturing wildlife. Their interest is further supported by our Discovery and Learning programmes, *The Zoo* television series, our links with organisations working with animals in the wild, and the long experience of the Zoo team. The global challenge to halt the decline in biodiversity, preserve the wild and conserve species is more urgent than ever before and, with the goodwill and trust of our visitors, Dublin Zoo is now in the enviable position of being empowered to foster change.

As Dublin Zoo consolidates its focus and becomes an important centre for conservation, we remain constantly aware of our ethical values and remain true to the founders' sentiments, that every animal is treated as an individual that is cared for with intelligence and compassion. The Dublin Zoo team including our council and volunteers are committed to making the Zoo a place where the animals are cared for to the highest standards and where our visitors can be inspired about wildlife while they enjoy a memorable day out. This new edition of our history by Catherine de Courcy is a wonderful opportunity to incorporate recent developments into a new record and celebrate the long tradition and history of Dublin Zoo.

Leo Oosterweghel, Director

Sigra, Sumatran tigress,
Dublin Zoo.

Preface

The new edition of Dublin Zoo's history arose from the combined need to reprint the original edition and the desire to bring the story of the Zoo up to date. In 2009, when the first edition was published, Dublin Zoo was still in the early stages of an ambitious developmental phase, which commenced with the 2006 master plan. The Kaziranga Forest Trail, the first animal habitat created under this plan, was opened in 2007, and the African Savanna was opened just before the original history went to print.

Since then the master plan with all of its complex layers has been implemented. Habitats inspired by real, wild places allow the animals to live in social groups and behave much as they would in the wild. The gardens, always a splendid feature of Dublin Zoo, immerse animals and visitors in a natural landscape. The animal care team follow international best practice and through their networks contribute to the development of animal husbandry, most notably in the care of the Asian elephants. And education, which had been at the heart of the Zoo since its foundation, is now delivered from several purpose-built spaces as well as being woven into every aspect of the Zoo's work.

When the first edition of the history was published nine years ago, there was limited public knowledge about conservation and other activities going on in Dublin Zoo. Today the situation is quite different with many very well informed visitors. *The Zoo* television series, which began broadcasting in 2010, has played a big part in this, as has the expansion of the Zoo's education programmes, the increase in the body of committed volunteers, and the rise of social media which, by 2019, allows the Zoo to communicate with over 380,000 people through Facebook, Twitter and Instagram. Through these channels, Dublin Zoo spreads knowledge about its mission, 'To work in partnership with zoos worldwide to make a significant contribution to the appreciation, understanding, and conservation of the natural diversity of life on earth.' It also remains an award winning venue for a family day out with well over one million visitors each year since 2011.

In its 188-year history, Dublin Zoo has remained open for 363 days a year (except in extraordinary circumstances), has attracted more than 55 million visitors and has as its governing authority a council composed of men and women with different interests who have ensured the continuity of the institution for nearly two centuries. This has given Dublin Zoo a rich social history. However in order to keep this book at a manageable length, a straightforward chronological approach has once again been taken in which the phases of development are identified with reference to the international context. As before, official records of the Zoological Society of Ireland form the backbone of the research with newspaper articles, and observations and recollections by Zoo staff, council members and visitors providing further insight into the Zoo's history. The 2009 history was divided into seven chapters and the structure in this new edition remains the same with Chapter 7 now covering the period 2000 to 2019. Chapters 1 to 6 have been edited down, although new material concerning the 1916 Rising, the MGM lion and the development of education has been included. Chapter 7 has been completely rewritten. The chapters are uneven in length with the final chapter being considerably longer than the others. This was to keep the book at a reasonable size while allowing a full overview of the developments in the Zoo since the year 2000.

Over 50 per cent of the photos in this edition were not in the previous book. These range from old prints and glass slides to recent images of animals and people in the Zoo. A photo of the Asian male elephant, Prince Tom, on a ship on the way to Europe in 1870 was sourced from the Getty Collection. A large collection of glass slides taken by J. Alfred Scott, a council member from 1907 until his death in 1926, was sourced in the Royal College of Surgeons Library Heritage Collection. Several of the images have been included in the book and I am very grateful to archivists Meadhbh Murphy and Mary O'Doherty for bringing them to my attention. The National Library extended its image catalogue online and some terrific photos from the early twentieth century and from the 1930s are now readily available. Several of these have been included. As with the last edition, photographer Damien

Maddock has been incredibly helpful in taking photos for the book and digitising old images in various formats from the Zoo collection, and I thank him for all of his help. For this publication, we are very fortunate to have a large collection of superb photos of Dublin Zoo animals, habitats, Zoo employees and volunteers, events and visitors taken since 2010 by Patrick Bolger, who takes many of the Zoo's photos for their press releases.

In 2018 the Dublin Zoo Marketing team organised a competition on social media to invite visitors to send in historical photos. Photos dating back to 1930 were received, each with their own story. I have included a number of these but for production reasons it was impossible to use them all, especially recent ones that would have gone into the final chapter. I would like to thank everyone who sent in photos, who spoke to me on the phone and who came to the Zoo to have photos taken, and I am only sorry that they could not all be included. I am also very grateful to all of the individuals, photo studios and institutions who have allowed me to use their photos. Full credits for these photos are found at the end of the book.

With the new research focusing on the last 20 years, I am very grateful to current and former members of the Dublin Zoo team for taking time to talk to me and helping me to identify animals, plants and people. Thank you to Paul O'Donoghue, until recently the Assistant to the Director (Animals and Grounds), Operations Manager Gerry Creighton, Animal Care Team Leaders Helen Clarke Bennett, Ciaran McMahon and Eddie O'Brien, recently retired Curator of Horticulture Stephen Butler, Marketing Manager Emma Kiernan, Head of Discovery and Learning Aileen Tennant, Retail and Visitor Services Manager Mark Bowes, Registrar/Research and Conservation Coordinator Sandra Molloy, Volunteer Coordinator Noreen Fitzsimons, recently retired veterinarian John Bainbridge, and keeper Brendan Walsh, who gave me access to his historical archive.

Although little information has been added to the earlier chapters, I needed help with identification of animals and people in newly acquired photos and I am very grateful to retired senior curator Gerry Creighton (senior), who identified animals, and to keeper Garth de Jong who identified reptiles. Although Chapter 6 (1980–2000) has been edited down, additional information has been included and I was fortunate to have had enlightening interviews with the first education officer in Dublin Zoo Elizabeth Sides, with John Barry of Management Support Services who has been involved with human resources management in Dublin Zoo since the 1980s, and with founding Park Manager at Fota Wildlife Park Sean McKeown, and his colleague, the late Carmel Conroy. I am also very grateful to long-serving volunteers, Maeve McDonald, Mary Neville and Mary Marsh, who gave me an insight into the early years of the volunteers.

A heavily illustrated book such as this, particularly with the emphasis on the recent times, required a lot of assistance from the dedicated Marketing Team. I am very grateful to Suzanne O'Donovan, Aoibheann O'Flynn and Aoife Keegan for helping to gather together many of the great illustrations in Chapter 7. I am also especially grateful to Marketing Manager Emma Kiernan for her considered advice and support.

With all of the small details involved in publishing this book, the support of the Zoo's administrative staff was critical to its success. I am especially grateful to Jennifer Kenna, Personal Assistant to the Director, who gave me an enormous amount of practical help at every step of the way and I thank her for her patience and assistance. I would also like to thank Aoife Murphy and Gemma Doherty at the Zoo's reception.

Outside the Zoo, numerous people helped me in bringing this book together. I would like to thank Con Collins, Breda McEnaney, and James McGowan for their advice and assistance. I would especially like to thank Anna de Courcy and Rose Foley for their skilled copy-editing, advice and support, Kate McGowan for help with the index, and Sandra Molloy for comments on the final proofs. The designer, Karen Carty of Anú Design, has been immensely forbearing in making all of the minor adjustments requested to ensure that the book looks its best; I would like to thank her very much for her patience. And I would like to thank Karen Hughes of PrinterTrento for her support in achieving the final look of the book.

And once more I would like to thank the director, Leo Oosterweghel, for the invitation to write this history. His enthusiasm for zoo history generally and the history of Dublin Zoo in the context of the present day and future vision is inspiring. It has been a pleasure to explore and present the wonderful achievements of the Dublin Zoo team over the past 20 years in the context of the Zoo's 188-year history.

Children participating in a Discovery and Learning programme in the Wild Space, Dublin Zoo.

Chapter 1

Dublin Zoo: The Beginning
1831–1860

Summary

Dublin Zoo was first opened to the public on Thursday, 1 September 1831. The collection was small and included a wild boar, deer, macaws, cockatoos, and a pair of emus. The site was also small, a four-acre plot by a lake in Phoenix Park. But the vision of the men who founded the Zoo was far-sighted. At a time when cruelty towards animals was commonplace, they wanted to promote greater respect for all living creatures. Philip Crampton, the surgeon-general and mastermind behind the Zoo, said in his foundation speech:

> To cultivate a kindly disposition towards animals, it is only necessary to know them. An intimate knowledge of their characters, disposition, and talents, may... tend to abate that spirit of cruelty and selfishness which leads us to seek amusement in the suffering and destruction of the most beautiful, harmless, and happy of sentient beings.[1]

As anatomists, physicians and zoologists, many of the founders had a professional interest in studying animals alive and dead. Together they created a zoo with very little money and limited knowledge about how to manage exotic species. The early years were difficult but they persevered, even bringing the Zoo through the Great Famine. The situation improved in the 1850s, and by 1860 Dublin Zoo was flourishing. More than that, it was firmly established as an institution of the city of Dublin.

The foundation

The plans for the Zoo began in May 1830 when Philip Crampton gathered together a well-connected group

ZOOLOGICAL SOCIETY.

THE Zoological Garden, in the Phœnix Park, under the patronage of his Excellency the Lord Lieutenant, will be opened for Visitors on THIS DAY, THURSDAY, SEPTEMBER 1st, at Nine o'Clock in the morning, and will not be closed until a late hour in the day.

All persons are to be admitted for Six Pence each.— They are to write their names at the gate.

A member who has paid his subscription, and two of his friends coming with him, are admitted free of expense.

Members are also allowed to purchase transferable tickets.

The Committee request that visitors may leave their stick and umbrellas at the gate.

And that children may be kept from approaching too near to the bars which confine the animals.

J. Pim, Esq., 41, Dame-street, continues to receive subscriptions and donations.

The first day's receipts will be given to the Mendicity Association.

Left: Sir Philip Crampton (1777–1858), surgeon-general and founding member of the Zoological Society of Ireland. **Above:** Advertisement announcing the opening of Dublin Zoo on 1 September 1831.

of doctors, academics, scientists and Irish nobility to create the Zoological Society of Ireland. The concept of a permanent collection of animals run by a society of volunteers was new in the 1830s. For centuries wild animals, including elephants, lions, tigers and rhinoceros, had been displayed at fairgrounds and in pleasure gardens around Europe. The atmosphere of these show grounds was generally boisterous and the animals were one of the many side shows there to surprise and entertain. At the same time, royalty and nobles kept private menageries. In 1779 one of these, the royal collection in Vienna, was opened to the general public becoming the first urban zoo in the modern tradition. In 1793 during the French Revolution, exotic animals from the royal collection in Versailles and other private collections in France were transferred to the care of the scientists at the Jardin des Plantes in Paris. In December 1794, the menagerie was opened to the public, so making it the second zoo in the modern tradition.

But it was the third zoo, London Zoo, on which the original Dublin Zoo was modelled. London Zoo was opened in 1828 by the Zoological Society of London, a scientific organisation devoted to the study of animals, alive and dead. The collection was brought together to support research and was only open to members. The novelty of meandering around well-kept gardens in genteel company while looking at exotic animals made London Zoo immensely popular and membership of the Zoological Society soared. Carlow zoologist and politician, Nicholas Vigors, was a co-founder of the Zoological Society of London and it was he who provided Philip Crampton with advice and support on setting up Dublin Zoo. The approach was broadly similar to London Zoo in that Dublin Zoo was created as a permanent collection of animals close to the city with well-tended gardens and a management committee composed of society members. The major deviation from the London model was that from the very beginning Dublin Zoo was open to non-members with the declared intention of spreading knowledge of and respect for animals among the populace. At the time there was much discussion about banning blood sports including bull-baiting, a cruel activity in which a bull was tied to a post, provoked and attacked by trained dogs. Philip Crampton spoke about how a zoo could make a difference:

> The boy who, day after day, shares his cake with the bear who runs up a pole to receive it... will scarcely go out of his way to see such an animal baited and torn to pieces by infuriated dogs, set on by... the most abandoned of men.[2]

The entrance fee for non-members was sixpence, which was not a cheap day out but at least it removed the exclusivity that defined London Zoo.

The original lodge in Dublin Zoo and home to the superintendent. It was demolished in 1868 to make way for Society House.

Building the Zoo

The Zoological Society of Ireland had influential friends, one of whom was the Lord Lieutenant, the Duke of Northumberland. The duke gave the new society the use of four acres in Phoenix Park to display the collection. He had no authority to grant government property to a private organisation but, with a gift of animals coming from London Zoo, the Department of Woods and Forests had little choice but to honour the generosity of the Lord Lieutenant. However, until 1894 the land was only on loan and the Society could have been forced to vacate it with two months' notice on the request of government officials.

The gift from London formed the nucleus of the collection. Other donations were received over the following years and by November 1832 Dublin Zoo had 56 mammals including 15 monkeys, and 72 birds, among them two passenger pigeons, a once-common species that became extinct in the early twentieth century. The carnivorous animals included a wolf, raccoons, a hyena, leopards, foxes and a bear. Mr R. Drewitt, an experienced animal keeper from London was appointed superintendent in 1832 and was given accommodation in the one existing building on the site, a lodge formerly occupied by a deer keeper and his family.[3]

The animals were housed in cages and paddocks. A row of open sheds was built along part of the northern wall of the site, shallow sections of the pond were enclosed, and paddocks were created using rough timber uprights and bars. Night shelter for the ostriches and emus was created with boxes and the deer were given thatched-roof barns. The buzzard and peregrine falcons were chained to trees outside. A warm house with glazed windows and a stove was built; it was only 24 metres long and four metres wide but all of the animals believed to require heated accommodation were kept in it. These included the leopards, the hyena, several monkeys, a squirrel, a pelican, parrots, macaws, a kestrel hawk, herons, birds and tortoises. Accommodation was rudimentary and it is probable that smaller animals were kept in cages, one on top of the other.[4]

A design master plan for Dublin Zoo was drawn up by Decimus Burton, a renowned English architect who had designed London Zoo. The small plot of land occupied by the Zoo was on the high ground to the east side of the lake, close to where Haughton House

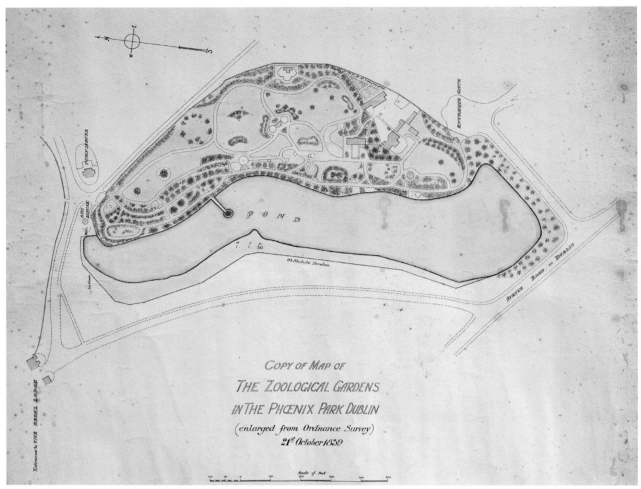

COPY OF MAP OF

THE ZOOLOGICAL GARDENS

IN THE PHŒNIX PARK DUBLIN

(enlarged from Ordnance Survey)

21ˢᵗ October 1839

Above: The 1832 design of Dublin Zoo by English architect, Decimus Burton. This copy was made in 1839. **Left:** A pelican was purchased from a ship's captain in 1832. The bird had reportedly struck the sail of his vessel in the Dardanelles in a fog and had fallen to the deck stunned. Costing £14.14s, it was the first large expenditure on an animal in Dublin Zoo. Image from the *Dublin Penny Journal*, 1836.

hill and across the water to the park beyond. Burton suggested that small ponds be formed at the north side of the lake, where it was shallow, so that waterfowl could be displayed in different categories.

and Zoorassic World in the Roberts House now stand. Burton's design used the lake as the focus of the Zoo and he incorporated the west side of the lake, ignoring the fact that the land was not occupied by the Society.[5] He placed the entrance in its current position on the south side because it was convenient to the city. Most of the animals were placed on the higher ground, which was about eight metres above the level of the lake. The shrubs and under wood around the lake were to be cleared, allowing visitors beautiful views down the

Early days

The Zoo was moderately successful at first. The Zoological Society of Ireland, with the patronage of the Lord Lieutenant, had 283 subscribers by 1833 including bishops, dukes, earls and lords along with army officers, doctors and academics. A few women were listed as members in their own right, including the Countess of Glengall and a 'Miss Edworth', who was probably the Irish author Maria Edgeworth, a friend of Philip Crampton. As the Zoo was largely funded by

Clockwise from top left:
The entrance lodge designed
by council member and
architect, William Deane
Butler, and built in 1833 for
about £30; The elephant
rented by Dublin Zoo in 1835;
Llama in Dublin Zoo. Images
from the *Dublin Penny
Journal*, 1835–1836.

subscriptions and donations from members, the list of subscribers was posted at the front gate to entice new members into this distinguished company.

Over the following years, lions, a tiger, a puma, monkeys, various birds including an expensive pelican, and other animals were added to the collection. A bear pit with a climbing pole was excavated. During the summer of 1835, the Society rented a ten-year-old elephant for £100 a month from a travelling animal keeper called Atkins. An Asian rhinoceros was also rented for a short period. In spring 1836, London Zoo gave Dublin a female elephant on condition that Dublin returned the skeleton of the animal after it died. Following the death of the elephant in 1842, London changed its mind and allowed Dublin to keep it. After a series of public demonstrations about the elephant's anatomy, the skeleton was presented to the Royal Dublin Society for its natural history museum.

By the mid-1830s, when the city's population was about 200,000, over 40,000 people were walking, riding or taking carriages out to the Zoo each year. The gardens were laid out with beds of flowering plants, summer fêtes were arranged and military bands played on the lawns. The keeping staff wore dark green velveteen waistcoats and jackets, with buttons adorned with a harp. Sticks and umbrellas had to be checked in at the gate, probably to prevent visitors from tormenting the animals by poking them.[6]

The council of the Zoological Society of Ireland

The first management committee of the Zoological Society of Ireland was composed of 15 members. Three

Clockwise from top left: The Indian rhinoceros rented by Dublin Zoo in 1835; Lion in Dublin Zoo; Kangaroo in Dublin Zoo. Images from the *Dublin Penny Journal*, 1834–1836; The Deambulatorium financed by Philip Crampton in 1838 to provide the big cats with an outdoor space to exercise.

years later it reorganised itself, taking as its model the Geological Society of London. A council was created with a president, several vice-presidents, a secretary, a treasurer and 15 members, with the option to add another six. This core group of men supervised all of the work involved in creating the Zoo in the early days. At least once a week, summer or winter, they made their way by carriage or horseback to the Zoo where they ate a hearty breakfast by the open fire in the superintendent's lodge. They received a report from the superintendent and then went on their rounds, giving instructions about the design, construction, modification and planning of fences, cages, paths, paddocks and buildings. They hired and fired staff, arranged for the purchase or acceptance by gift of animals, worried about the budget, and discussed animal care.

Little enough was known at the time about the diets and husbandry needs of wild animals and few in the Zoo besides Superintendent Drewitt had any experience in dealing with these species. Consequently the mortality rate was high in the early years. As the animals died, their carcasses were quickly claimed by council members for dissection and study, and inclusion in one of the small zoological museum collections in the city at the time.

This council as designed by the founders was to continue to run the Zoo up until 2008 with much of the work devolving onto the honorary secretary and other office holders. The composition of the council often made it unwieldy because, with former office holders remaining on, it might number as many as 30 people. From 2008 the number of members was limited to 12. Although their direct involvement in the management of the animals and the grounds had faded out in the 1980s, the Zoological Society council is still the governing authority of Dublin Zoo.

Coronation Day

In November 1837, the young Queen Victoria agreed to become patroness of the Zoological Society of Ireland. At the annual general meeting in May 1838, the council announced that the Society would henceforth be called 'The Royal Zoological Society of Ireland'. On her Coronation Day, 28 June 1838, the Zoo was opened with free admission from midday until 6.00 p.m. It was estimated that 20,000 people visited, an extraordinary number, if accurate, to accommodate on a four-acre site. By 1838 the membership privileges had been extended and members' children under 12 were being admitted free of charge. Six pence was still prohibitive to the general public, although it was possible that they were able to see the animals from the perimeter fence, or by crossing the lake where it is shallow, or even by eluding the staff. The Zoo was particularly vulnerable to non-paying visitors on Sunday mornings as the gardens did not open until 2.00 p.m.

Financial woes

For all the interest in the new zoo, the Society's financial status was very unstable. Subscriptions and gate receipts did not cover the expenses of setting up a zoo and council members had to lend money to pay wages and food bills. In December 1838 the honorary secretary, Robert Ball, wrote to London Zoo about the situation in Dublin:

> I regret to say that with all efforts we can make (save converting our garden with a puppet show or place of carousel) we cannot gain sufficient public support to enable us to add to our collection to any great extent. It not infrequently happens that at this time of the year that our receipts at the door do not exceed £3 in the week.[7]

By July 1839, the situation had deteriorated further. Ball wrote to London Zoo asking if they would be interested in purchasing Dublin's carnivora; at this stage, the Zoo was feeding beef to the lion, tiger, puma and leopard, rather than the cheaper horseflesh, which was being fed to the other carnivora:

Robert Ball, (1802–1857), honorary secretary of the Society from 1837 until his death. 'With him the prosperity of the Zoological Gardens was a personal concern... His motives for this exertion were a benevolent desire to make that science as available as possible to the widest circle of the public.' *Saunders News-Letter* 6 May 1857.

> It is believed [the sale] will not only effect a very considerable reduction of expenditure but prove acceptable to the public, who perhaps find their curiosity with respect to carnivora sufficiently gratified by the more frequent exhibitions at theatres and other places... our stock of carnivora is small but it is particularly healthy, we have a very fine tigress, a lioness, jaguar, pumas and leopard (all save the jaguar extremely gentle).[8]

London Zoo agreed to buy the jaguar. Superintendent Drewitt, tired of the council's interference in the everyday business of running the zoo, resigned and bought the lion and tiger, which he set up in an animal show elsewhere in Dublin. There was still enough in the Zoo to attract visitors but the novelty was wearing thin and the council was unsure how long they could maintain the expensive institution. Even London Zoo, the most fashionable place to be seen in the early 1830s, was experiencing a drop-off in numbers.

Penny entry

In 1840 the Dublin Zoo council made the momentous decision to drop the price of admission to a penny on

Sundays. The magnitude of this decision is difficult to comprehend from a modern perspective but in 1840 the Royal Zoological Society of Ireland was essentially a club for the wealthier people of Dublin. Two members of council, Robert Ball, honorary secretary, a civil servant and curator of the Zoological Museum in Trinity College Dublin, and James Haughton, a corn merchant and social reformer, wanted the Zoo to provide 'healthy and instructive recreation for the well-conducted people who are busily occupied during the week'.[9] Some members raised objections, concerned that the general public would destroy the exclusive atmosphere of the Zoo. However the plan went ahead and from 1 May 1840 Sunday entry was dropped to one penny making it affordable to the working classes of Dublin, who worked six days a week.

Cheap entry was an immediate success. From May 1840 to April 1841, 81,404 people visited the Zoo on a Sunday. Their behaviour was monitored closely and there were no problems, no injuries to animals, no bad behaviour and no drunkenness. In 1842, the council reported:

> Though the majority of visitors to the Gardens were admitted at the low rate of one penny... the Council believe that this, so far from lessening the value and importance of the Society, shows it... as a valuable aid to the enlightenment of the people.[10]

Soon afterwards the council began to reduce the entrance charge to a penny on selected public holidays, especially around Christmas and Easter.

Albert Tower

With the success of penny Sundays, the council looked to the 1840s with renewed optimism. In 1844, London Zoo sent Dublin a giraffe named Albert, which had been born there three years earlier. He was a hardy animal and made the journey across the Irish Sea with no ill effect. In exchange, Robert Ball sent London a two-toed sloth and a new species of tiger cat.[11]

The arrival of the giraffe prompted the construction of a new animal house. Known as Albert Tower, this was the first solid structure to be built in Dublin Zoo. It was designed by George Wilkinson, the Society's honorary architect and a member of council, and was intended to house a giraffe, an elephant and a camel in separate compartments. Wilkinson put a lookout tower on the top of the building. When the full cost of the structure was worked out, a scaled-down version of Wilkinson's plan was agreed upon. The foundation stone was laid on 24 May 1845 by the president of the Society, the Duke of Leinster, in the presence of the Lord Lieutenant. The stone was hollow and two glass jars were placed in it with a series of items, including an illustration of the building, a ticket for a lecture in the Royal Dublin Society's premises in Leinster House, Kildare Street, and a ticket for a promenade in the Zoo. The stone with its contents emerged in May 1962 when Albert Tower was demolished to make way for a hippo house.

Albert the giraffe attracted 132,000 visitors in 1844–1845, more than half the estimated population of Dublin at the time. Nearly 99,000 were penny visitors, and it was not until 1857 that that number of visitors was again recorded.

The Great Famine

The presence of the giraffe cushioned the early effects of the Great Famine on the Zoo. But by 1847, the impact was unmistakable as visitor numbers dropped and the cost of feeding the animals escalated. The council announced that they were no longer using food that could be consumed by humans. Horsemeat, rough barley and other food unsuitable for human consumption took the place of potatoes, bread, oats and butchers' meat. Small quantities of poor quality Indian corn were fed to the fowl. It was difficult to maintain a supply of hay and straw as prices rose, and Francis Buckley, the superintendent, struggled to get reasonable prices at the markets.

During the Famine years, animals died of distemper, heart disease, accident and other causes. The goat was destroyed by the bison, young bloodhounds died at birth, a golden eagle on loan was killed by an otter, an arctic fox was 'destroyed by the others', a kangaroo had a swollen face and died, baboons died from diarrhoea, an African eagle escaped when the roof was blown off his cage, an otter escaped through the weir while another was killed by his mates, and an Egyptian goose got into the bear cage and was killed. The elephant died unexpectedly from an inflammatory disease. Only a black bear was recorded as having died for want of food, although it is possible that some of the animals died from being given poor-quality or inappropriate food.

Financially the Zoo was in a desperate situation. In 1847, the council warned that if it could not liquidate the debt of the Society, they would have to decide

8

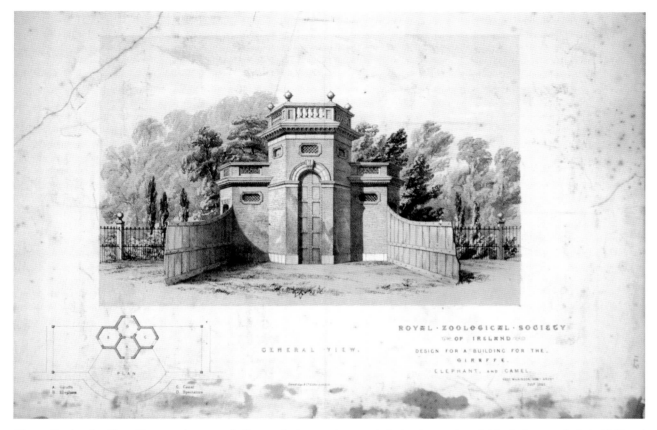

Above: Design for Albert Tower to house a giraffe, an elephant and a camel. A simpler version of this design was built in 1845 and remained in place until 1962. **Below:** Group photograph taken 1855 (l-r): Sir Dominic Corrigan, Dr George Hatchell, Jacob Owen, Dr Robert Ball, Sir Francis Brady, Prof. George Allman, Patrick Supple, James Lowe (superintendent), Welsh (carpenter), John Supple, Patrick Rice.

whether they could face another winter with the cost of fuel constantly rising and gate income declining. They pleaded with members to pay their subscriptions and somehow they managed to carry on, probably with financial help from council members. By 1849, there were six staff, the superintendent, a clerk who also worked as the gatekeeper and watchman, two keepers and two gardeners. Robert Ball, in his capacity as director of the Zoological Museum in Trinity College, purchased the carcasses of animals and this provided a small income for the Zoo.[12]

Rebuilding in the 1850s

As the country began to recover after the Great Famine, the Zoo recovered with it. The International Exhibition on Leinster Lawn in 1853 attracted nearly one million visitors, many of them tourists, between May and October. The Zoo benefitted from this influx and recorded a remarkable 114,000 visitors in its reporting year 1853–1854. The gardens were cleaned up, decaying cages, stables and sheds were rebuilt, and new animals acquired. Then, in 1854 the Society received an annual government grant in response to yet another plea for assistance. The council

had justified its request by pointing out that crowds of people 'bearing the marks of weekly toil' were provided 'with a resource from which they go home refreshed and with quiet minds, fitting them to work happily for the next week at their several occupations'.[13] The government accepted this argument and pledged an annual grant of £500 a year, which provided a measure of stability to the Zoo. Further concessions could now be made. Penny entry was introduced on evenings after 6.00 p.m. during the summer months. Governesses were to be allowed in with members and the members' children and, if they had been identified, they could bring the member's children to the Zoo by themselves. Art students were to be admitted free of charge, as were a sizeable number of charitable groups.

In 1854, an aquarium with 15 tanks was opened in Dublin Zoo close to the perimeter fence. It incorporated the latest knowledge in keeping fish and aquatic plants together in a tank and aerating the water. The aquarium was stocked with many varieties of seawater and freshwater fish, and with sea anemones, zoophytes and crustaceans procured from the coasts of Howth and Dalkey. Plants and rocks were used to furnish the fish tanks, and mirrors were concealed in one of the larger tanks to throw light on the fish and the rockwork from below. Frost caused some difficulties the following winter but overall the system of aerating the water proved very successful.

Irish lion industry – the beginning

With the government grant and 95,000 visitors in 1855, the council felt confident that they could afford the initial cost and ongoing expense of keeping lions once more. In 1855 they purchased a pair of young lions for £285, which was more than their entire income from subscriptions in 1854. The council was satisfied that the staff had the skills to keep these animals; a leopard had lived in the Zoo for over ten years and a puma and a jaguar had been living there for four years. The lions were reportedly taken at Natal, in southern Africa, and were named Natal and Natalie. In 1857, Natalie had a litter and this marked the beginning of what became known as the 'Irish lion industry'. Before he died in 1864, Natal had sired a total of 42 cubs, ten of them with Natalie. The lions became a useful source of income for the Zoo as the cubs could be sold or exchanged. In 1860, one lioness was exchanged for a rhea, a king vulture, a peccary and £10 worth of monkeys. In 1861, four female cubs were exchanged for a lioness, a polar bear, a black bear, a Nilgai, a boa constrictor, a rhea, and several smaller quadrupeds and birds.

As the first generation of the Dublin Zoo's council moved towards retirement, all of the elements required to keep this institution going were in place. Its future would depend on a new generation of voluntary council members to carry on the work of the founders, and on Society members to support it financially.

Visitor numbers 1832–1860. The peak in 1845 was due to the arrival of Albert, the giraffe.

DUBLIN ZOO – AN ILLUSTRATED HISTORY

Chapter 2

Consolidation
1860–1895

Summary

Happily for Dublin Zoo the second generation of Royal Zoological Society of Ireland council members was enthusiastic and capable. Led by the formidable academic the Reverend Professor Samuel Haughton, son of James Haughton, this generation consolidated the position of the Zoo. By 1895, when Haughton retired from the council, the Zoo had increased in size, had several substantial animal houses, and its tenure of the land in Phoenix Park was secure. Many exotic animals had been seen in the Zoo at some stage, the breeding of lions had gained international recognition and the staff skill in caring for the animals was well developed.

And always the focus was on bringing people closer to animals so that they would learn about them and appreciate them. Cheap entry was extended to evenings, Christmas week and other times convenient
to workers and their families. The pleasant atmosphere was maintained with tasteful entertainment, well-kept gardens and council members always on alert for any signs of misbehaviour.

Dublin Zoo in 1860

In 1860 the area occupied by the Zoo was still confined to the east side of the lake and the Society was still on two months' notice to vacate it. There was a carnivore house, an aquarium, several aviaries, cages, small paddocks, the thatched entrance lodge, the superintendent's house, the imposing Albert Tower and a tent-like structure, which housed a valuable plesiosaurus fossil, which had been donated by Philip Crampton.[1] The collection of animals was varied enough to appeal to visitors, who used every opportunity to interact with them, mostly by feeding them, which was acceptable at

Above: Entrance to Dublin Zoo, 1860s.

Bear perched on the climbing pole in the bear pit, which was built in 1832. Photograph taken c.1934.

The Reverend Professor Samuel Haughton (1821–1897), a portrait by Sarah Purser. Haughton was a powerful and influential member of the Society council from 1860 to 1895. He was a geologist, physician, zoologist and academic. During this period he used his exceptional management skills, fundraising ability and renowned wit to consolidate the position of Dublin Zoo.

the time, but also by teasing, poking or even throwing stones at them, which was definitely not acceptable. The more popular mammals were the African lions and their cubs, a pair of Bengal tigers, polar bears, the dog-faced baboon and the many monkeys. The aviaries in the Zoo contained a variety of native and exotic birds including cockatoos, parakeets and peafowl. Ostriches, emus and rheas were kept in paddocks, while ducks, geese and swans were encouraged to nest on the lake. The aquarium contained cuttlefish and pike, and the reptile collection included tortoise, salamanders and green lizards. The animals were looked after by a small team including the superintendent, Mr Lowe, four keepers, Patrick Rice, Thomas Flood, John Supple and James Gorman, as well as a gardener and a carpenter.

The council members continued to meet for a cooked breakfast in the parlour of the superintendent's lodge before getting down to business. In 1860 there were 29 council members, many of whom attended the meetings regularly; those who attended the fewest meetings were liable to be replaced. At their meetings acquisition of animals by purchase, donation or exchange formed a significant part of their agenda. By now zoos had been established in numerous cities around the world, including Amsterdam, Antwerp, Berlin, Calcutta, Marseille, Melbourne and New York and, over time, the council used this network to exchange animals and information. The council also discussed the health of the animals, the condition of their cages and enclosures and the Zoo's financial position,

Albert Tower designed for the giraffe, elephant and camel. Photograph taken early twentieth century.

which was invariably poor. When an issue required further investigation or management, a committee or subcommittee was set up to do the job.

During the week, at least one council member was on duty in the gardens to monitor the health of the animals, ensure the visitors behaved themselves and to check on staff. They recorded their observations in a notebook, issuing instructions on everything from the diet of the bison to the flooring in the lions' cages. Sometimes they clashed with each other, one countermanding another's instructions. When physician Samuel Gordon purchased a cage that would allow the porcupines some fresh air, geologist Joseph Beete Jukes came in a few months later and ordered that the cage be enclosed, concerned that the animal might die from the cold.

The visitors

Nearly 75 per cent of Zoo visitors in the early 1860s came in on Sundays at the cheaper rate but still some Society members were not happy with their presence. When, in 1861, Dominic Corrigan, president of the Society, proposed to members that admission to the Zoo after five o'clock each summer evening would be reduced to a penny, Dr John Kinahan was one of several who objected. He complained that he had seen animals being teased, tree branches broken, and flowers cut. But other members declared that they had experienced nothing but good humour and good behaviour on Sundays. The motion was carried, yet members continued to raise the conduct of penny visitors until Corrigan said, at the annual general meeting in 1863, that there was no need to discuss the subject any more: 'It was, to his mind, paying but a poor compliment to the citizens to say that they behaved themselves'.[2] Bad behaviour did, of course, occur, but it was not restricted to Sundays or evenings. In 1864 a man was convicted and fined for throwing stones at the bear. A little while later, keeper Patrick Rice retrieved a wheelbarrow-full of stones from the bear pit; one of the stones had hit the male bear in the eye, blinding him in that eye.

Society parties and promenades

The members the Royal Zoological Society of Ireland were vital to the continued development of the Zoo through their subscriptions, donations, voluntary work and influence. In order to make membership appealing, the council organised social events, often with the Lord Lieutenant and his entourage in attendance. The summer promenades, as they were called, were especially popular. The staff worked hard to prepare the gardens for the summer season with colourful flower displays, tended walks, and mowed lawns. Fashionably dressed crowds gathered to feed the monkeys and watch lion cubs play while military or police bands or the band from the Hibernian School would play lively music on the lawn. The practice began in the 1830s but by the 1860s, the promenades were so well attended that mounted police were on hand to ensure there was no congestion with the horse-drawn traffic outside the Zoo.[3]

Expanding the Zoo

Since the 1830s, the council had made several attempts to get permission to erect a fence on the west side of the lake and therefore incorporate it fully into its boundaries. Their motivation was to protect the western access to the Zoo rather than acquire extra space. Phoenix Park deer often swam across the water, ate shrubs, plants and flowers, and upset the animals by going close to their cages. Human predators and their dogs were also a problem, particularly when they raided the waterfowl nests on the lake. In addition Samuel Haughton, now honorary secretary, wanted to charge for ice skating on the lake and create an income for the Zoo during the winter months; when the lake froze over, it provided some of the best skating in Dublin.

The council petitioned the government for permission to fence the perimeter of the lake and in 1864 it was granted. To the council's surprise, the government surveyor placed the new boundary at the top of the rise above the lake. This gave the Zoo a stretch of land on the west side of the lake that they had not expected or even asked for.[4] A public appeal to support a 'fence fund' allowed the council to complete the iron-railed fence.

The following winter was bitterly cold and the lake froze for two weeks. Penny entry on Sundays was suspended so all visitors other than members had to pay the full admission fee. At times there were up to 300 men, women and children skating on the ice. In January 1865, the ice cracked and five young men ended up in the water. They were saved by cork fenders attached to ropes and were hauled out safely. The skating continued with Zoo staff and ten policemen on hand to sweep the ice and to help out if the ice cracked again.

In anticipation of another such incident, the Society purchased two folding ice ladders, two hand ladders, two cork belts and two stands marked 'dangerous'. The next ice season was not until 1866–1867. After nearly four weeks of good skating conditions the ice cracked and 21 people ended up in the water at the south end of the lake, near the entrance. The water was then estimated to be about five metres deep. The council reported that all were saved but 'two gave much trouble to restore them after being landed'. Superintendent Edward Carter and his wife who were living in the lodge looked after the unfortunate skaters. A good profit was recorded from the skating season that year.[5]

The animals' living conditions

The cold weather of the 1860s was not good for the animals and in many cases their accommodation was inadequate for very low temperatures. Stoves were placed in all of the houses. Matting was put on the glass roof of the reptile house but even with two stoves in operation, the keepers struggled to keep the temperature up. The boa constrictors were rolled in blankets and put by a fire; later they were placed in warm water. A Barbary ape, suffering from the cold and in poor condition, was rubbed with fresh butter but had to be destroyed a few days later. In 1865 the big baboon became ill; it was said that he was missing his hot morning and afternoon tea that the wife of a former superintendent used to make for him. Although he was given a medicinal mixture of ginger cordial and laudanum, he died and his body was sent immediately to Samuel Haughton in Trinity College for dissection.[6]

The most serious winter loss was Natal, the male lion purchased in 1855. In 1864 he was unwell with rapid and labouring respiration. He was given every attention possible. His den was enclosed with straw and boards and he was administered regular doses of beef tea and whiskey punch. His health improved briefly and, as the word went out that he was ailing, large crowds came to see him on the Sunday before he died.

The cold was not the only problem and animals' accommodation was becoming increasingly inadequate in other respects. The collection was growing as more species became available and the keepers' husbandry skills improved. Conditions became cramped and problems arose, especially where pairs of animals were kept together. An old black female bear was very weak after being knocked about by the old male and was moved in with younger bears. A female ostrich broke her leg when she was chased by the male. The need for new enclosures was becoming urgent but, without substantial financial help from the government or a

benefactor, there was no question of doing anything other than patching up what was there and finding cheap ways of making the animals comfortable.

The rhinoceros

The Zoological Society of Ireland had influential friends living in countries where exotic animals could be acquired. In 1863, Sir Charles Trevelyan, a British colonial official based in Calcutta, bought an Indian rhinoceros for Dublin Zoo. He kept it in a local collection until, in mid-1864, the young animal was placed with a consignment of animals destined for London Zoo. He arrived in Dublin in August 1864. The acquisition cost the society £160, which was a considerable saving on the commercial price of £400. From the beginning, the rhino was unsettled and prone to fitting. The council recommended a strict diet

including boiled rice, bran, milk and a tonic powder. As the rhinoceros' health improved, potatoes were added to his diet in order to reduce his allowance of hay, which was expensive. Although calm for much of the time, he was also unpredictable and on at least one occasion he attacked Patrick Rice, his keeper.

In spring 1865 the rhinoceros became unwell and one afternoon in April, he became especially agitated. It emerged that he had a prolapsed rectum. Samuel Haughton, several medical men on the council and the veterinary surgeon gathered. With the rhino clearly in excruciating pain, a potion including castor oil, opium, aromatic spirits of ammonia and spirits of turpentine to kill worms was administered with tepid water. It did not help much. Haughton sent a telegram to Abraham Bartlett, superintendent of London Zoo, asking for suggestions but the unhelpful response was to treat the rhinoceros as they would a horse suffering from the same cause. Back in Dublin, the keepers and the council members did what they could.

Eventually, late in the evening, the rhinoceros quietened down, probably, Haughton suspected, of exhaustion rather than any impact from the medication. Keepers John Supple, Thomas Flood and James Gorman stayed during the night to care for him but at four in the morning, the rhinoceros died. The Royal Dublin Society offered £15 for the carcass, another offer of £16 was received, while Haughton offered £19 on behalf of Trinity College and won the bid. The post mortem by Haughton assisted by Hugh Ferguson, a veterinary surgeon, found a fermenting mixture of hay and whole Indian corn in the stomach of the animal. They concluded that 'death was caused by the improper administration of Indian corn'. Haughton was annoyed because Indian corn was not supposed to be part of the animal's diet. Patrick Rice was blamed and his wages were reduced from 15 shillings a week to 12 shillings and sixpence per week for a year for his part in causing the death of the valuable animal.[7]

Death of John Supple

In November 1867, keeper John Supple was bitten by a reticulated python. The python, which can reach ten metres in length, kills by strangulation and is not venomous. However 55-year-old John Supple reacted fatally to the bite and died of congestion of the lungs. The council contacted the superintendent of London Zoo to see if they had been at fault in believing that the snake was not venomous. Abraham Bartlett said both he and his keeper, Holland, were frequently bitten by a python but it only caused a smarting, unpleasant sensation. Bartlett did agree that someone could be frightened to death if bitten by the snake. The council paid the funeral expenses and employed his son, Patrick, who was then working for a lithographer in Middle Abbey Street. Patrick Supple continued to work in Dublin Zoo until his death in 1913. His son, Jack Supple, started at the Zoo in 1902 and became famous as the keeper in charge of the chimpanzee tea parties; he retired in 1961.

Capital works

For years Samuel Haughton and the council had used their influence to request financial help from the government and in the late 1860s their persistence paid off. This was a time of expansion in the sciences and arts in Dublin and Sir Henry Cole, Secretary to the Department of Science and Art, was granting capital

Edward Carter, superintendent from 1865–1880, with his wife, Maryanne, and eldest daughter, Maryanne, outside Society House, their home in the Zoo, built 1868. The ground floor room to the right of the picture was used for Society council meetings.

funds to Irish institutions; however, no money was to be provided for ongoing expenses. Using this grant, the existing superintendent's lodge was demolished in 1868 and a new home was completed on the same site. The large room on the ground floor was designated for the council's use while the superintendent and his family lived in the rest of the house. It became known as 'Society House' and in 2019 is still used as the director's home. A new monkey house was erected, the water supply was improved, and several cages were removed or replaced. And in 1869, a new aquarium and a carnivore house were completed.

The carnivore house, more commonly referred to as the lion house, was opened in May 1869 with a ceremony the modern reader can only marvel at. A newspaper described the scene of the lions being transferred from their old quarters to the new house:

> The usual method of transporting such animals was adopted on the occasion. Ladies as beautiful as Ariadne and as virtuous as Úna, each holding a beefsteak on a toasting fork, preceded each leopard and lion to its new habitation. The leopards and lions followed as if in duty bound and are now on view in their new house.

Another procession involving beef, music and the lions was advertised for the following Thursday on the occasion of the first promenade of the season:

> At four o' clock precisely the band will strike up the 'Roast Beef of Old England' and a procession headed by a wheelbarrow containing shins of beef will be formed, and proceed to open the new lion house in the gardens. The inhabitants… were successfully 'decanted' into their new residence on Monday last. The members of the Dublin public that had not the advantage of witnessing the striking procession of ladies and lions on Monday last are earnestly requested to favour the procession on tomorrow with their presence.[8]

The trams

For all the parties, bands and ice-skating that gave members and their guests a sense of belonging to an exclusive club, three-quarters of the visitors came on Sundays, bank holidays and during the summer evenings when entry was a penny, soon to be raised to two pence. At that time, most would have made their way to the Zoo by foot, although records suggest that a bus company came into the Phoenix Park. In 1870, private companies were in discussion with Dublin Corporation about laying down tramways around the city. The successful company was told that it was to add an additional route from Sackville Street (O'Connell Street) to the Botanic Gardens and Glasnevin, and to the park gate and Zoological Gardens by the North Circular Road.[9] The new tram line was operating by 1876. Despite requests from the Zoological Society council to have the line extended to the entrance to the Zoo, the line ended at the North Circular Road gate to the Phoenix Park.

Prince Tom

In the summer of 1871, the Zoo acquired an elephant on loan from a circus for several months. The elephant's feet had reacted badly to the 'sloppy carbonate of lime' on the country roads, so the circus was glad to allow it to rest in Dublin Zoo for a while.[10] It was a great attraction. Later that year the Prince and Princess of Wales visited Dublin Zoo where their attention was drawn to the lack of an elephant in the collection. At the prince's instigation, his brother, the Duke of Edinburgh, donated to Dublin Zoo an elephant he had recently brought back from India. Named Prince Tom, the male Asian elephant was clearly well trained and was soon giving rides and performing the usual tricks expected of a zoo elephant at the time. The following newspaper report was written in May 1872:

> Perfectly docile and harmless, [Prince Tom] is left almost to his own guidance and walks about the gardens with an apparent consciousness that he is the cynosure of the place. He generally keeps near the handsome kiosk where refreshments are dispensed, to which he is one of the best customers. If a visitor gives him a penny, which he receives with courtly grace, he at once enters the shop, at least he inserts his huge head and fore quarters, which nearly fill up the little place, hands the coin to the attendant and takes a bun in exchange. His greatest pleasure seems to be to receive a sixpence when, after purchasing his cake, he returns the change to the donor with a low salaam. A ride upon

Asian elephant named Prince Tom on a ship bound for Europe. He lived in Dublin Zoo from 1871–1882.

his back round the garden is a treat to the younger visitors.[11]

A month later, a different story emerged. When the Duke of Edinburgh was visiting Ireland, he asked if Prince Tom could be brought around to the Vice Regal Lodge so he could have a look at him. The council had to refuse the request. Walking the elephant down the road to their next-door neighbour should have been no problem if the report in the newspaper about this docile elephant walking among visitors was true. However, the council had it on record that there had been a few incidents involving Prince Tom's temper and did not want to risk him walking outside the Zoo.

Prince Tom continued to entertain visitors. A bathing pool was excavated for him which, according to a contemporary report, was large enough for him to step into and, 'Once in… put his great head under water and began plunging, and rolling, and snorting in gigantic fashion'. During the summer, his bath became an event to observe during promenades and sixpenny entry days. One newspaper described a bath in which Prince Tom filled his trunk with muddy water and sprayed the crowd of visitors who had gathered around to watch: 'Pretty, delightful, and trembling the ladies dashed about where

they could and what are called bonnets were mutually examined with intense anxiety'.[12] Prince Tom did not have access to his bath on cheap entry days.

In September 1873 a visitor named John Wall instigated legal proceedings after he claimed he was injured by Prince Tom. He wanted medical and other expenses; he also recommended that the elephant be locked up when the gardens were open to the public.[13] The council rejected his claims. The following spring, Prince Tom attacked another visitor and injured his keeper, who was trying to protect the visitor. The council decided to keep the animal inside his house on Sundays when the Zoo was busiest. In September 1874, a keeper, who is not identified, was reported for being drunk, and the elephant was reported for behaving in a disorderly manner at the same time. The outcome of that incident was that Prince Tom was confined to his house and a small enclosed space outside, where he remained from then on.

In 1882, Samuel Haughton announced to the Annual General Meeting that Prince Tom was dying. He said,

> [Prince Tom] was a very ill tempered, ill conditioned elephant long before he left India, and killed his keepers on the way

Above: Lioness and cubs, 1885. **Left:** Thomas Flood and council member, probably Thomas Maxwell Hutton, at the entrance to the lion house built in 1869. When the building was extensively refurbished as an extension to the Roberts House in 1909, the decorative stones from the door surrounds were used in the reconstruction. They can still be seen in the exterior wall of Zoorassic World.

> although they took the best care of him, and the animal had at last broken down in health and would not live long… He was being fed on every delicacy, sugar, rice balls, carrots and potatoes, all which he ate with pleasure.[14]

Prince Tom died in January 1882. His body was drawn on a float to the Trinity College Department of Anatomy where, with shears, ropes and pulleys, he was studied and his skeleton placed in the Zoological Museum in the college.

Irish lion industry

By the 1870s Dublin Zoo's international reputation for breeding lions was well established. Between 1857 and 1876, 92 lions had been born in the Zoo, of which 71 had reached maturity under the supervision of keeper Patrick Rice. Dublin's lion cubs had the reputation of being strong, healthy and a good size, and could therefore command high prices from animal dealers.

home and at home, and he had several times attempted to kill persons in the gardens. Greatly against their will, the council was therefore obliged to restrain his exercise and to lock him up. This affected his health,

As was normal practice for animal dealers at the time, Dublin Zoo took no responsibility for the cubs once they left the Zoo. But there were few complaints about the quality of the Irish cubs and they tended to travel easily to their new owners. Sales, swaps and partial swaps were arranged with dealers and other zoos, and the lion cub industry became an important factor in the solvency of Dublin Zoo during this period.

Tourists came to the Zoo especially to see the lions. In summer 1870, there was a report in the *Brooklyn Daily Eagle* about Dublin's lions, in which the author said that, 'I shall never see a lion again without pleasing remembrances, and the belief that I have patted his father or mother upon the neck in the Dublin gardens.' In December 1878, former president of the United States of America, General Ulysses Grant, came to the Zoo to visit Charlie, an especially large lion. Standing with Samuel Haughton, the former president lit a cigar and stood for a period contemplating the celebrated lion. Afterwards he signed the council's minute book.[15]

Pygmy hippopotamus

In 1873, another of the Zoological Society of Ireland's friends in distant lands sent Dublin Zoo a particularly

Top: Cheetah with keeper Patrick Supple, 1893. **Above:** Stuffed pygmy hippopotamus in the Zoological Museum, Trinity College Dublin. The young animal died in 1873, a few hours after arriving at Dublin Zoo.

rare animal. It was a young pygmy hippopotamus, which had been captured in Sierra Leone after the death of its mother. At the time, Dublin Zoo's council claimed that it was 'hitherto an almost unknown animal'.[16] In March 1873, Patrick Supple was sent to Liverpool to collect the small creature, which was estimated to be about eight weeks old and weighing 25 pounds. Unfortunately the loss of its mother and the journey to Europe took its toll and despite the best efforts of Patrick Supple, the pygmy hippopotamus died a few hours after it arrived in Dublin Zoo. Alexander Macalister, director of the Trinity College Zoological Museum, acquired the remains and undertook a dissection, the results of which were published in the transactions of the Royal Irish Academy. The skin of the animal was preserved and stuffed and this little creature is on display in the Trinity College Zoological Museum.

Education

Education was still at the heart of Dublin Zoo and the focus of the council's work. Public education was achieved by opening the Zoo at cheap rates, providing as diverse a collection as they could assemble and labelling the enclosures, and this was considered sufficient for the general public at the time. Occasionally lectures were held but the subjects were often esoteric and generated little interest. However one talk at the Zoo should have attracted a great audience. In 1862, Paul Du Chaillu and his stuffed gorillas visited Ireland and the council invited him to speak in the Zoo. Du Chaillu had returned to Europe from an expedition to West Africa with 20 stuffed gorillas as well as skins, skulls and skeletons and claimed that he was the first European to have seen the animal. Charles Darwin's *Origin of the Species* had been published in 1859, sparking widespread debate about the validity of his theory of evolution based on natural selection. The arrival of Du Chaillu's stuffed gorillas fuelled the debate with many claiming that they were fakes and Du Chaillu was an impostor. The visit of Du Chaillu to Dublin Zoo in May 1862 was well advertised and a military band was engaged to play on the lawn. But it rained and very few people turned up. Du Chaillu offered to waive his fee but the council insisted on paying him.

Dublin Zoo's second stated educational objective – to supply comparative anatomists, physicians and zoologists with the opportunity to study foreign animals – was more successful. Many members of council had a professional interest in the study of animals. Their advice on diet and husbandry was very useful at a time when little was known about how best to keep exotic species in an alien climate, and there was probably a lot of experimentation with the help of the keepers on how best to look after specific species. When an animal died, the carcasses usually went to one of the scientific bodies for study and analysis. The skeletons or skins of many Dublin Zoo animals are still to be found in Irish museums. The more important animals, the elephants, rhinoceros, giraffe, the primates and the big cats, were keenly sought after and bidding for the carcass was lively. When, in 1885, an orangutan arrived at the Zoo, the zoologists did not wait for the great ape to die before bidding for its carcass. Professor Daniel J. Cunningham of the Trinity College Department of Anatomy, offered £4 for the animal provided it was sent to him the moment it died. Haughton countered this offer by bidding £5 but stressed that it was unlikely to die soon. Patrick Supple was given charge of the valuable animal, named Sinbad and told 'on no consideration whatever to feed the ourang-outan but at regular hours and on specified food and never to open the glass case for anyone, not even member of council'.[17] On one occasion, in 1887, Sinbad fell ill and after an anxious time, his convalescence was announced and he was allowed 'to receive visitors from 1 to 3 o'clock p.m. daily'. He lived for nearly four years in the Zoo, which was a testament to Patrick Supple's skill. Sinbad died of a disease that was similar to typhoid fever: 'His near kinship to ourselves was thus borne out to the end, seeing that he succumbed to a complaint which is supposed to be peculiar to man,' wrote an anonymous

council member.[18] Samuel Haughton secured the body for the Trinity College Zoological Museum.

Death of Thomas Flood

Keeper Thomas Flood was killed by a red deer stag in the Zoo in October 1880. He was 45 years old and had been with the Zoo for 22 years. He had cleaned the enclosure and was leaving when the animal attacked him. The investigation into the experienced keeper's death was inconclusive. Either Thomas Flood had not bolted the gate properly or had not moved out of the inner enclosure quickly enough after finishing the cleaning. Whatever the cause, the stag fractured his skull, broke seven ribs, and cut his hands. Despite his injuries, Flood managed to push the stag back into its enclosure and shut the gate. When the superintendent Edward Snow and keeper George Bristow got to him, he was barely conscious; as they lifted him up, he said, 'I think I'll walk'. He died shortly afterwards.

Haughton praised Flood for finding the strength and courage to secure the animal despite his great injuries and called for donations for the family. Thomas Flood's son, Christopher, then aged 22, was employed in the Zoo with the promise that he would not be put in charge of the red deer. Christopher Flood became a much-loved lion keeper in Dublin Zoo, working in the carnivore house for over 50 years.

Elephants: Rama and Sita

Early one morning in March 1882, two young elephants from Burma arrived in Dublin and were walked along the quays to the Zoo. It was only seven o'clock in the morning but 400 to 500 people emerged to accompany them. Named Rama and Sita, they were believed to be 'so gentle… that they will take from the hand of the tiniest child its little offering of cake or sweet meat without causing the infant the slightest alarm'.[19] But a month later, they escaped from their house and, trumpeting loudly, broke through a number of barriers and destroyed the pigeon house. When they were finally locked up they were still agitated. Behaviour like that did not stop the council from allowing them out to mix with visitors. A contemporary report describes a typical scene:

> The elephants daily go forth drawing an immense van along the roads of the Phoenix Park in order to strengthen their muscles and supply them with a good appetite for dinner. Our children, of course, get many a ride on the docile beasts who, with equal equanimity, convey a bevy of giggling servant maids along the shaded walks and back to the starting point, stalking silent and dignified under all the giggling.[20]

Captain Harrington, an elephant trainer, was employed to train the animals and their keeper, James McNally. In 1890, Rama died suddenly and lay in his house where he had fallen for 22 hours. When Professor Daniel J. Cunningham arrived to retrieve the body for a post mortem in Trinity College, rigor mortis had set in. It took 50 policemen and the keepers to squeeze

Asian female elephant, Sita, with keeper James McNally in c.1900.

the body through the door of the elephant house. The post mortem indicated that the elephant had suffered from advanced pneumonia and in that weakened state, enteritis had killed him.[21]

Financial problems

By the 1880s, as Samuel Haughton's period of influence began to draw to a close, the management of the Zoo seemed to slide. Visitor numbers were dropping off and balancing the budget became even more difficult. From 1884, the Zoo opened at midday on Sundays, an extension of two hours, yet visitor numbers continued to fall away. Being largely reliant on entrance fees for income, it became more difficult to maintain the animals and their facilities. Haughton suggested that the Zoo get a licence to sell alcohol but the idea was dismissed by his colleagues. He organised side shows, including four dog shows and an odd event in which the Cavill family, a father and three children, performed swimming and aquatic feats in the lake dressed in red wetsuits. Small amounts of money were raised but these poor attempts to bolster the Society's funds only drew anger from disgruntled members. A

Crowd outside the open-air aviary, which was erected in 1893.

letter to the *Daily Express* signed by one calling him or herself 'Gloomy decay' gives an indication of what was going wrong:

> It is most distressing to observe the steady and downward movement of these our once famous and national Zoological Gardens… It strikes me the root of the evil is not far to seek. The management is rotten, so to speak. Therefore, the whole concern is decaying.

A zoological garden is not the place for scientific experiments and the pampering of the fancies of a few. It should be for the pleasure and instruction of the public… We do not want our Zoological Society to become a company of scientific experimentalists, a dog show committee, or yet purveyors of skating to the public, but we want it to be what it was intended to be, and what its grant from Government is for, a society to increase

The zebra house, late nineteenth century.

and cultivate in the public mind an interest in objects of natural history.

Some time ago, an eminent naturalist, speaking to me of our society's gardens, said he had come to the conclusion that it was now but a place kept up to provide skins and skeletons for the Trinity College Zoological Museum… The fact is that the animals are not thriving but are rapidly diminishing, and what still remain in the gardens are not kept so as to interest or attract the public.[22]

Part of the problem was Haughton himself. He was a renowned public speaker and clearly enjoyed a verbal skirmish. So when members tried to challenge him at annual general meetings of the Society on conditions in the Zoo, Haughton met their challenge, sometimes agreeing with them, sometimes disagreeing but always

adding a comment that made the audience laugh. He also used the Society's meetings to express his support for Home Rule and his antipathy to British rule in Ireland. His speeches were very entertaining and he received a lot of support for his political opinions but it did not contribute to the better management of the Zoo.

In July 1890, Francis Guy was appointed superintendent to succeed Edward Snow. Guy was an experienced animal keeper, having owned a large private collection on a 20-acre site at Raworth Park in Suffolk. When he arrived in Dublin, he was appalled at the standards of husbandry, especially with regard to the feeding of animals:

Sometimes the animals were overfed, and sometimes three parts starved. The food was never the same either in quantity or quality, and there was scarcely a trough in the whole gardens in which food could be placed.[23]

He planned to introduce reforms by strategic firing and hiring of staff but was prevented in doing so by the council. The council members were, by now, used to managing every aspect of the work at the Zoo and their continued interference frustrated Francis Guy so much that he threatened several times to resign.

Seven months after taking up his contract, Francis Guy did resign. The final row was over the opening of the refreshment room in winter. The council wanted him to renovate it and keep it open during the winter months, even though there were less than 40 visitors a day. Income from the refreshment room was supposed to supplement the superintendent's modest salary but Guy insisted it was a waste of time and effort. He had a private income and did not need the money. The council pointed out that it was part of his contract. In the end he resigned. Haughton praised Guy for the expertise he had brought to the Zoo, especially in relation to the monkeys' diet: 'So good was the dietary now that, should anything happen to him, he would prefer going to the monkey house rather than to the workhouse,' Haughton was reported as saying.

But for some members, the resignation of an experienced zoo manager was the last straw. Abraham Shackleton, a former member of council, was quoted in the *Daily Express* as saying,

> the council had not been as efficient as it might have been… Their principal duty appeared to be to eat a good breakfast at the gardens and, perhaps that was right for there were some members of it who were fit for little else.[24]

A Captain H. Church wrote:

> It is with a sad heart that I am bound to confess that the wholesale denunciations hurled at the defenceless head of the council of this Society are richly deserved. It is painfully apparent to the most casual observer that a more deplorable state of things could scarcely exist, and I much fear that unless the people of Dublin wake up from their lethargy at once it will be too late to rescue our 'Zoo' from being numbered with the past.[25]

Another report that appeared in the *Evening Telegraph* just after Francis Guy's resignation, was headlined 'The Zoo controlled by opponents of reform'. It suggested that many of the animals were mangy, that birds were diseased, the collection in the aquarium was laughable, several cages were empty, and labels were missing. It summed up by saying, 'There was an air of squalor and inattention suggestive of approaching bankruptcy.'[26]

Thomas Hunt, a senior constable who had lived near the Zoo for 25 years, was appointed to succeed Francis Guy as superintendent. He had a calming influence and seemed capable of settling conflict. Reference to troubles at the Zoo disappeared from the newspapers.

Entrance to the Zoo, late nineteenth century.

Death of Francis Wright

On Christmas Eve 1891, there was a tragic accident in which a 17-year-old man from Limerick died as a result of being mauled by a brown bear. Francis Wright had been feeding sweets to the bear when he turned around to look for his six-year-old brother. The bear grabbed his arm and pulled him over. Keeper Christopher Flood heard a shout and ran down to the bear pit where he found Francis Wright struggling with the bear. The superintendent and keepers were alerted and ran to his assistance. Thomas Hunt fetched the revolver and reported that, as he approached with the loaded weapon ready to shoot, Francis Wright was rescued. The young man was taken to Dr Steevens' Hospital but died shortly afterwards. His father called into the Zoo early in January to see the place where the accident had occurred and thanked the staff for what they had done in trying to save his son. Extra bars were placed in the bears' cage.

The end of an era

Before this period so closely associated with Samuel Haughton ended, there was a significant occurrence for the future of the Dublin Zoo in the Phoenix Park. In 1894, the agreement by which Dublin Zoo was granted 'permissive occupancy' of the site in Phoenix Park was drawn up. This gave the Zoo greater security on the site than before. An additional strip of land on the south side of the lake near the entrance was also granted. The Zoo itself might have been in a poor state but it had consolidated its position with this agreement. At the 1893 annual general meeting Samuel Haughton said that he had been:

> brought into the Society by Robert Ball many many years ago... and [I] found that [at the time] it was the opinion of a great many, including Sir Philip Crampton and Sir Dominic Corrigan even, that the Society could go on no longer. But Dr Ball said, 'The Society must not die; we must make another strenuous effort and another.' This went on and the Society was not allowed to die, but had gone on increasing and flourishing.[27]

After that meeting, Haughton retired. In 1895, Professor Daniel J. Cunningham was appointed secretary and immediately proposed a programme of improvements. In 1897, the death of Samuel Haughton was announced. The council responded by opening a subscription and building Haughton House in his honour.

Visitor numbers from 1861–1895. The peak in 1871 was due to the arrival of Asian elephant Prince Tom.

Chapter 3

Expansion and War
1895–1922

Summary

With the change in leadership, the politics of the council shifted and became noticeably more loyal to the crown. Gone were all references to Home Rule and instead the council took every opportunity to express its loyalty to Queen Victoria and, on her visit to Ireland in 1900, it presented her with an address declaring its 'deep devotion' to her as sovereign. In 1898 Field Marshal Lord Roberts, commander-in-chief of the army in Ireland, was appointed president of the Society. He was an odd choice as he attended few meetings and the role of president was a demanding one. However, under his guidance Dublin Zoo entered a golden period, benefiting directly from the colonialism that had supported so many other European zoos during the nineteenth century. Visitor numbers soared, reaching 260,000 during 1907 when the Dublin Exhibition was held in Herbert Park, and this allowed the Zoo to get new buildings, more animals and better facilities for visitors as well as generate a lively social atmosphere.

Programme of improvements

Under the direction of Professor Daniel J. Cunningham, honorary secretary to the Society, a major programme of improvement and renovation commenced in Dublin Zoo in 1895. The aquarium was turned into a reptile house, an up-to-date rockery for exotic goats was built on the west side of the lake, and a house for camels and llamas was constructed. The aquarium had been a source of embarrassment for some council members; it was the only high-temperature building in the Zoo and it housed the retiles, the chimpanzee, the cheetah, Malayan bears and other animals that required constant warmth. Cunningham pointed out that visiting naturalists were 'staggered at the omnium

Clockwise from top left: Camels and visitors at Albert Tower; Donegal wild goats in their enclosure on the west side of the lake, built 1896. Photograph taken c.1910; Entrance to the Zoo, early twentieth century.

gatherum which they encounter in this room, at this association of reptile with the man-like ape'.[1] The display of animals by classification was the more usual way for public zoos to display animals at this time and, to a large extent, Dublin Zoo went along with this approach: the lions, tigers and other big cats were kept in the lion house, birds were kept in the aviary and many of the primates were in the monkey house, but the lack of money meant that there was sometimes a mixture in one exhibition area. The experience for visiting naturalists was not helped by the fact that the chimpanzee was one of the more popular animals in the Zoo and the small room where this omnium gatherum was displayed became very stuffy and crowded on Sundays.

Adapting the old aquarium to house the reptiles was a good solution. An alligator pool was placed in the middle of the house, which allowed the animal to submerge the whole of its body under water for the first time in Dublin. Small, heated compartments with plate-glass fronts were installed for snakes and lizards at one end of the room, and a pool for cormorants and penguins was created at the other end. The decision was made not to have venomous reptiles in the collection until the keepers became accustomed to handling snakes.

The goat enclosure, completed in 1896, was the first animal exhibit to be placed on the west side of the lake. It was also the first enclosure in the Zoo to incorporate the new, theatrical style of zoo architecture that was being developed in Europe. Using blocks of undressed stone, a rockery with uneven surfaces was created for the ibex, angora and other foreign goats. It was designed to represent a naturalistic environment,

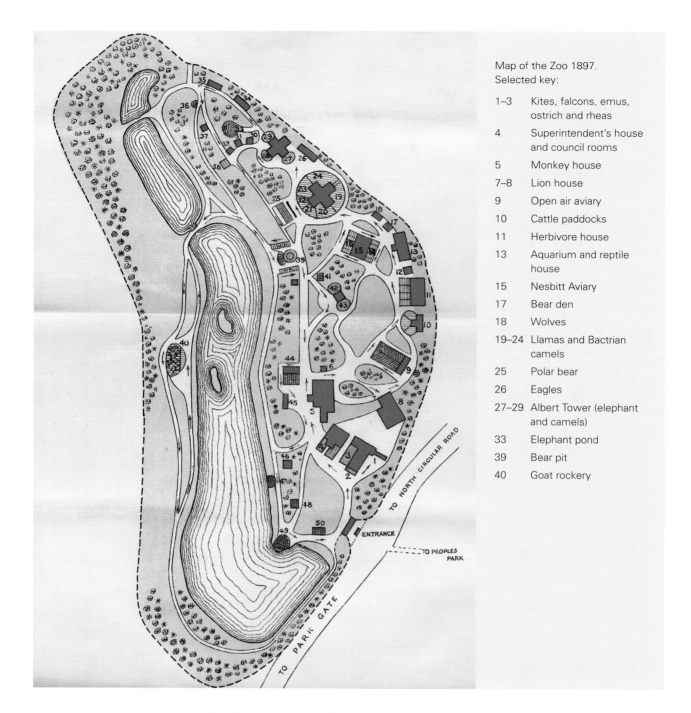

Map of the Zoo 1897.
Selected key:

1–3	Kites, falcons, emus, ostrich and rheas
4	Superintendent's house and council rooms
5	Monkey house
7–8	Lion house
9	Open air aviary
10	Cattle paddocks
11	Herbivore house
13	Aquarium and reptile house
15	Nesbitt Aviary
17	Bear den
18	Wolves
19–24	Llamas and Bactrian camels
25	Polar bear
26	Eagles
27–29	Albert Tower (elephant and camels)
33	Elephant pond
39	Bear pit
40	Goat rockery

provide a more interesting exhibit for the public and improve conditions for the animals.

The animal collection

As soon as he took office as president, Lord Roberts wrote to Irish-born officers who were serving with the British imperial army around the world and asked them to send animals back to Dublin Zoo either as a donation or for transportation costs only. In July 1898 a Colonel Walters wrote from central India saying that he had received Roberts' communication and promised to bring animals for the Zoo on his return to Ireland. In September, a major in Hyderabad wrote about sending tiger cubs to Dublin. Over the coming years, up to 80 separate donations were made each year. Some donations were from traditional sources close to home, but others were sent from the British colonies and included meerkats, leopards, baboons, caracaras and pythons. Roberts also communicated with celebrated animal collectors such as Walter Rothschild, who presented several giant tortoises from the Galapagos Islands during this period.

Meanwhile the lions continued to produce cubs at

a steady pace, providing plenty of interest for visitors in the lion house. Visitors could get a ride on Sita the elephant, feed the monkeys and take refreshments in the room run by Thomas Hunt, the superintendent. A new bicycle shed was erected by the entrance and, following a petition by a photographic society, the rules restricting photography in the Zoo to members were relaxed and from 1898 anyone could apply to the superintendent for permission to take photos of the animals. The same year it was also possible to see the chough, a native Irish bird that was 'in the process of rapid extermination'. Nest robbing was blamed because the chough was considered 'the most engaging of pets'. Then, as the bird became rarer, there was an even greater demand for their eggs from collectors, who gambled on the bird becoming extinct. When the Zoo went to look for some choughs to include in the collection, a collector boasted that he had sold more than 300 eggs that season. The Society petitioned officials in several coastal counties to protect the bird.[2]

Haughton House

Haughton House was built in 1898 to honour Samuel Haughton and his long and valuable service to Dublin Zoo. Designed by Laurence McDonnell, the two-storey building had an elegant tea room upstairs with an ornamental fireplace, a small kitchen and pantry, and a library. The upper floor was accessible via two external staircases, which led to balconies that provided splendid views over the Zoo. This floor was for the exclusive use of members and would, the council hoped, attract new members who could retreat here on busy summer days or take refreshments by the fire on cooler days. During the summer, members were permitted to hold private parties on the balconies provided they brought their own servants, refreshments and appliances.

The ground floor of Haughton House was, strangely, used to accommodate animals in a series of cages with outdoor areas. While sheltered animal accommodation was needed in the Zoo, it was not an ideal situation. There were numerous complaints from members about the smells drifting up into the tea rooms, especially in warm weather. Nevertheless the animals remained until 1938 when the ground floor was converted into a public café.

Lord Roberts

Although Frederick Roberts attended few council meetings as president of the Royal Zoological Society of Ireland, his contribution was pronounced. Besides arranging for so many animals to be sent to Dublin, he took a keen interest in the management of the Zoo. On a walk around the Zoo after a council meeting in May 1899 he raised the crucial but hitherto unmentioned subject of public lavatories in the Zoo. There were public conveniences of some sort because Roberts suggested that they be improved, but what they were the records do not tell us. Certainly there was a lavatory in Society House, which was only available to the council, and there were facilities for members in

Scene from the west side of the lake in the early twentieth century.

Haughton House, built 1898.

Haughton House. There was also the small building known as the 'Victorian Toilet' outside the entrance to the Zoo but with a steadily increasing number of visitors, the need for improved facilities was critical.

Towards the end of 1899, Lord Roberts' son, Lieutenant Frederick Hugh Roberts was killed in action during the Boer War. Roberts, now 67 years old, immediately took up command and left for Africa, sending the council a note together with a picture of himself for the archive and information about the finalisation of the donation of two tiger cubs from His Highness the Nizam of Hyderabad. In March 1900, as he awaited the surrender of Johannesburg, he wrote to the council approving the annual report and checking on the progress of snow leopards, which he had arranged to be sent to Dublin.

Keeper James Kenny was also in South Africa at the time. In May 1899, the council had asked Lord Roberts if he could recommend a young retired soldier to manage the new animal enclosures in Haughton House. James Kenny, who was selected for the position, had been a rough rider in the 8th Hussars. In January 1900, he re-enlisted and went to South Africa; the council guaranteed that his position would be available to him on his return. Thomas Hunt was asked to keep an eye on his wife and family during his absence and an allowance was given to Mrs Kenny. Some years later,

James Kenny became Dublin Zoo's elephant keeper and held this position until his retirement in 1940. His son, Jimmy Kenny, succeeded him.

Roberts House

In 1895 Queen Victoria, patron of the Royal Zoological Society of Ireland since 1838, donated a lion to Dublin Zoo, which was named Victor in her honour. During her visit to Ireland in 1900 she spent an hour being driven around the Zoo looking at the animals. She promised Dublin more animals if they became available and she donated £25 towards the construction of a new lion house, which was to be built in Lord Roberts' honour. When she died in January 1901, the council went into mourning, postponed the annual general meeting and trimmed the first pages of the annual report in black. Her successor, Edward VII, agreed to be patron to the Society.

The new lion house, named the Roberts House, was also designed by Laurence McDonnell. Costing over £4,000, it was the finest of Dublin Zoo's animal houses and the only one that emulated the elaborate houses that could be found in wealthy zoos around the world at the time. Constructed in red brick, it was adjacent to the 1869 lion house. The official opening of the house took place at a formal garden party with 1,700 members,

Clockwise from top: Council members with head lion keeper Christopher Flood (4th from right) at the opening of the Roberts House, 1902; Interior of the 1902 Roberts House. The bench was designed to allow visitors to stand on it during lion feeding time; Interior of the 1909 extension of the Roberts House, incorporating the 1869 lion house. The Roberts House is now home to Zoorassic World.

Above: Lion in the Roberts House. Left: Field Marshal the Right Honourable Earl Frederick Sleigh Roberts (Lord Roberts) (1832–1914), president of the Society from 1898 to 1902. Roberts was awarded the Victoria Cross following action during the Indian Mutiny; he served in Abyssinia and Afghanistan, was commander-in-chief in India 1885–1893, in Ireland 1895–1899, and in South Africa 1899–1900.

guests and military officers in May 1902. The Lord Lieutenant, the Earl of Cadogan, ceremoniously opened the door of one of the outdoor dens and five young lions were let out to get their first experience of an open air enclosure.[3]

The animal accommodation in the Roberts House was an improvement on the old lion house with much better light and better ventilation. The cages had curved bars overhead and a glass roof that allowed sunlight to filter in. McDonnell had gathered information about carnivore houses in Europe and America and had used the design of the lion house in Zoologischer Garten in Berlin for some of the internal detail. He devised a system to ensure that the animals could move from one part of the house to another, from indoor cages to outdoor, and to safe zones so that the staff could clean the cages.

Successive councils had been nervous about changing the living conditions of the lions for fear that it would disrupt the successful lion industry. Speaking at

Leopard in the moveable connecting cage in the 1909 extension to the Roberts House. The cage is still visible above the exit door in Zoorassic World.

the opening ceremony of the Roberts House, Daniel J. Cunningham, the honorary secretary, said:

> The old house, shabby and unsanitary as it is, pervaded as it has been by an aroma which certainly cannot be said to be that of Araby, has a remarkable history... Within that house 217 lion cubs have been born.

He said the council had been warned that if they removed the lions from the 'stimulating atmosphere of the old house and place them in the pure air and well-lighted dens of the new house', that the lion industry would come to an untimely end.[4] They need not have been concerned – three lion cubs were born in September 1902, six in 1903 and nine in 1904.

Acquisition of a giraffe

Dublin Zoo's good fortune continued with the acquisition of a giraffe, thanks once more to the influence of Lord Roberts. Although giraffes had been well represented in European zoos and had bred reasonably well, Dublin had not acquired any since the death in 1847 of the London-born giraffe, Albert. In 1902 Colonel Butler, an Irish officer stationed in El Obeid, Sudan, acquired a giraffe and offered it to Dublin Zoo if the council would pay for its transport.

The council readily accepted the offer, insured the giraffe for £1,000 and made arrangements for its transport with Thomas Cook. It was an expensive undertaking and there were no guarantees that the animal would make it to Dublin. A head collar and a broad strap were placed around its neck and long ropes attached so that it could be controlled on the

Above: Camel with keepers, early twentieth century. Left: Arrival of the giraffe, 1902.

450 kilometre walk from El Obeid to Omdurman, a journey that took 13 days.

Once in Omdurman, Stanley Flower, director of Giza Zoo in Cairo, took charge. He was in the region with a team and a specially-equipped train to transport animals, including four giraffes destined for London Zoo. On the way the train was to pass under six bridges; the Dublin giraffe was so tall that a special

padded case with a sliding roof was constructed so that its head could be bent low enough to get under each bridge without incident. Eventually it arrived in Dublin and more than 9,000 people visited the Zoo the following Sunday. The giraffe died from pneumonia some months later. The carcass was sold for £30.

Shortly after the death of the giraffe a massive storm caused huge damage to buildings around the Zoo. The roof of the superintendent's house was blown off and Thomas Hunt spent an uneasy night wondering which of the animals might have escaped. The carnivores and bears were secure but many of the birds had escaped. As the estimate for repairing the buildings came in, so did an offer from Sir Reginald Wingate, the Sirdar of the Egyptian Army, to present two young giraffes and a lioness to the Zoo. Again the Society would have to pay for the transport. Faced with a choice of acquiring the

valuable animals or repairing the buildings properly, the council chose to take the giraffes and lioness and patch up the buildings as best they could. When the giraffes arrived the following August, the crowds poured in. A special house was prepared to protect them from the cold during winter. A glass screen was fitted and two radiators connected to a new boiler were placed inside the shelter to keep the temperature above 50°F (10°C).[5] The male died the following April of blood poisoning arising from an accident; the female lived on until 1909, growing taller and requiring the roof of her house to be raised so she could stand comfortably. She died suddenly when, it was believed, she had an attack of colic that caused her to throw herself violently about and fracture her jaw when she fell. It was many years before Dublin received another giraffe.

The elephants

When the period covered by this chapter began, Dublin Zoo had one elephant, a female called Sita. James McNally had been a keeper in the Zoo since at least 1873 and had looked after Sita since the mid-1880s. In February 1897, while still considered 'perfectly tractable' and not showing any 'vicious tendencies', Sita destroyed the wall of her house by butting it with her head. The wall had been rebuilt with brick and cement and a further buttress outside to strengthen it. A few months later, on a Sunday in May, a large crowd had gathered around Sita and were offering her pennies to buy biscuits and buns. When she was passing the biscuit back to a man who had given her a penny, another person in the crowd offered her something. According to official report:

> In its anxiety to get this [other offering] the animal pushed its trunk out across [keeper] McNally's chest and his feet slipped out from underneath him and he fell backwards... Unfortunately in the fall his head came in contact with the railing and it was somewhat severely cut. He never lost consciousness and was not on the ground for more than three or four seconds.[6]

Although McNally's head was badly cut, he insisted that the elephant did not pose a threat. No further action was taken and McNally and Sita continued as before – until a summer evening in 1903.

On 9 June 1903, McNally ordered Sita to kneel down so he could dress her foot. She had an overgrown toenail and was probably suffering pain every time she put her foot down. McNally, under instruction from a vet, was administering lotion to her foot. The usual procedure was that she would kneel on command but this time, according to McNally's 20-year-old son, John, who witnessed the event, Sita ignored James McNally's shouted instructions. Without warning, the elephant turned on her keeper, knocked him onto his side with her trunk and crushed his head with her foot. John McNally and another keeper called to Sita to fall back, which she did. The young man said the incident was over in about two seconds. The coroner ruled that James McNally's death was instantaneous and an accident. A subscription was opened for his widow and John McNally received a permanent job as an assistant keeper.

When closing the case, the coroner stated, 'the animal had met the fate usually meted out to animals guilty of deeds of this character. It had been destroyed that morning.' It was common practice in zoos at that time to destroy any animal involved in a fatal incident for fear that it indicated a new aggression towards keepers. Sita was given poison, cyanide of potassium, concealed in an apple but she spat it out. Colonel Sir Neville Chamberlain, of the Royal Irish Constabulary (RIC), offered to shoot her if an elephant rifle could be procured. The council sent to London for such a weapon and it arrived several days later. Chamberlain shot two bullets between her eye and ear and had five of the best shots in the RIC on hand to shoot at her shoulders if the head shots were not sufficient to kill her. The elephant rifle in Chamberlain's hands was adequate and Sita died instantaneously. Forty RIC men with three tug-of-war ropes took an hour and a half to pull the dead elephant into an outer enclosure where she could be dissected. The foot of the elephant was presented to the RIC in thanks for their work.[7]

Shortly before James McNally's death, the Duke and Duchess of Connaught had presented a 10-year-old elephant called Padmahati to the Zoo. Padmahati was now placed in the charge of James Kenny. An elephant trainer was engaged for a few weeks to train Padmahati to carry a saddle. In May 1904, she was ready to give rides and James Kenny was given a commission on the takings.

In 1907 Padmahati died from intestinal inflammation. Even with Lord Roberts' help, it was difficult to acquire another elephant. Instead, elephants were hired for the summer months each year until 1912, when a young female Asian elephant named Roma was purchased from Hagenbeck in Hamburg. Shortly afterwards, the Maharaja of Mysore honoured a promise to Lord

Roberts by sending a three-year-old female, Sandari, who had been trained in the Maharaja's private gardens and was ready to carry children. The council tried to sell Roma back to Hagenbeck but the elephant had grown considerably in the year she had been in the Zoo and was too large for Hagenbeck to sell on. Roma remained in Dublin.

August 1913

When industrial unrest erupted with the Dublin Lockout in August 1913, the council raised the question of staff wages. There was no indication of unrest in the Zoo at the time although working conditions for the staff had changed very little since the 1830s. All staff worked 70 to 80 hours per week, seven days a week and were given leave on request; the night watchman was the only exception – he worked 98 hours per week. There were no fixed closing times and, in summer, the Zoo might be open until 9.00 p.m. The Society regularly paid bonuses for success with breeding animals, organising events or undertaking extra tasks. The elephant keeper was allowed to keep any money he raised through selling buns for the elephant; it is also likely that other staff were allowed to keep tips and other small payments made to them by visitors. The superintendent was no longer responsible for running the refreshment room since Haughton House had opened, but his salary had been raised to compensate for the loss of income from this source. The Society paid small pensions to long-serving staff or to their widows.

Every year, in spring, the council undertook a wage review and raised the wages of a few staff each time. In 1913 the most senior keeper was on 26 shillings a week. In September, the council discussed staff wages again but, in the end, decided to leave it until their usual May review. They did, however, give an allowance to each member of staff to cover their liability to contribute under the Insurance Act.

The Great War

The social side of the Royal Zoological Society had expanded with the availability of Haughton House for functions. The garden parties had continued but now it was possible to entertain members and their guests to breakfasts and lunches. In June 1914, on the eve of the First World War, 64 members sat down at tables in Haughton House for the Ladies' Breakfast. Sir Charles B. Ball, the president and third son of the early honorary secretary Robert Ball, sat at the top of the long, central table, which was decorated with sweet pea, yellow daisies and other floral decorations. The menu included salmon, tomatoes, crumbed sausages,

Visitors watching the sea lions, August 1913.

Staff in the early twentieth century. Identifiable staff members include front row, seated, 3rd from left, Patrick Supple; 5th from left, Christopher Flood; far right, James Kenny. Middle row, 4th from left, Jack Supple. The men in cloth caps were probably grounds staff, the men in bowler hats were probably gate and office staff, and the man sitting in the front, centre, may be Captain Arbuthnot, superintendent from 1908 to 1911. The rest of the staff in the photo were probably keepers.

eggs, cold ham, mayonnaise, home-made jams and the speciality rolls for which Haughton House had become famous, followed by strawberries and cream. After breakfast, the guests wandered around the Zoo and visited the three-week-old lion cubs. The issues dominating the council meetings at the time were the problem of curtailing the growing rat population, deciding whether to create a small dark room where visitors could change plates on their cameras for a fee, and making plans to use a picture of the chimp called George on the advertising hoarding, which was to be hung by the railway companies in their various stations around the country.

Two months later, Britain declared war on Germany and the impact in Ireland was immediate. Young men left for the continent, food prices soared, the Horse Show in the Royal Dublin Society was cancelled and tourist travel was restricted. The council, copying the arrangements made by London Zoo, invited the wives and children of Irish soldiers serving abroad to visit the Zoo on weekdays free of charge. In September, the council made special arrangements with the manageress of Haughton House to welcome convalescing soldiers.

In the same month a staff member, L. Doyle, signed up; his job was kept open and his wife was to be paid during his absence. In October 1914 the council sent a letter to Joseph Nugent Lentaigne, a long-time member of council, with their condolences on the death of his nephew, Lieutenant Victor Lentaigne.

The shortage of tourists during the Zoo's busy season, particularly those from the Isle of Man who were notable for visiting Dublin Zoo in great number, caused a marked drop in income. The sharp increase in food prices and the loss of income from animal sales added to the council's financial woes but, in their annual report for 1914 they said:

> in the present terrible state of many European countries, we may be thankful that our chief trouble is a temporary shortage of money... Antwerp Zoo had to kill all of their larger carnivora for the sake of safety during recent bombardment of their city.

Dublin Zoo promised to help Antwerp restock their zoo on 'the return of happier conditions'.[8]

The council 1912. Front row (l-r): Prof. G.H. Carpenter, Prof. J. Alfred Scott, J. Nugent Lentaigne, Sir Charles B. Ball (president), W.E. Peebles, The Hon Justice Boyd, Dr MacDowel Cosgrave, Dr R.F. Scharff. Back row (l-r): Dr J. O'Carroll, Dr R. R. Leeper, Prof. A.E. Mettam, Prof. A.F. Dixon, Sir Frederick W. Moore, Col. Sir John Ross of Bladensburg, Dr George Scriven, Richard M. Barrington, Col. Sir Frederick Shaw, Col. Claude Cane, C.J. MacCarthy, Prof. J. Bayley Butler, H. F. Stephens, H.B. Rathborne.

At the outbreak of the war, Dublin Zoo had a very good collection of animals. Besides having two elephants, one of which was giving rides to children, they had a young gorilla named Empress, a young male chimp named Charlie and an orangutan named Sandy. These were joined in the monkey house in 1914 by a male hoolock gibbon, which had been a pet of the officers of a battalion of the Gordon Highlanders who had now gone to the continent. The Society claimed that, as far as they knew, the four types of anthropoids: gorilla, chimpanzee, orangutan and gibbon, had never been exhibited together before in any zoo.[9] Jack Supple was in charge of the precious apes and was credited with keeping these animals alive and in good health.

The lions were also a great attraction and were producing cubs regularly. Two well-known lions called Red Hugh and Fiona had cubs in the summer of 1914; they were all male, a 'remarkable and unusual preponderance of one sex', the council observed. There were five tigers in the carnivore house, including two cubs which had been a gift of Dr G. Combes, principal medical officer for the Cochin States, South India. Several well-known animals died during 1914, including two American black bears, two sea lions and a pair of snow leopards. Very few animals would be replaced before the end of the war.

As the war continued, managing the Zoo became more difficult. Donations of vegetables, leftover greens from the markets and seeds were willingly accepted as the cost of food for the animals increased. Fuel to heat the animal houses was also proving difficult to acquire but somehow they managed to get enough for the present. In April 1915 Dr Benjamin Ferrar, a medical doctor from Armagh and superintendent of the Zoo since 1911, accepted a temporary commission in the Royal Army Medical Corps and was on daily duty in the Dublin barracks of military hospitals. He continued to live in the Zoo and gave what spare time he had to his job as superintendent. There was no question of replacing him, although it was agreed that if he were sent out of Dublin on service, his wife, Isabella Ferrar, would take on some of his duties. The Ladies' Breakfasts were cancelled but lectures were held and a golf putting competition was organised, which was well attended.

Soldiers were frequent visitors to the Zoo. Men in uniform were allowed in for half price and those with wounds, convalescing or invalided soldiers were admitted with greater reductions or free of charge. Tickets stamped 'complimentary invalid soldiers' were given to council members to hand out to wounded soldiers personally known to them. Bands were organised to entertain the wounded men. In May 1915,

Orangutan, Bella,
with Patrick Supple, 1912.

the following announcement appeared in the *Freeman's Journal*:

By special request of some of the wounded soldiers who have returned from the battles around Ypres, the descriptive piece called the Battle of Ypres... will be repeated at the band promenade at the Zoological Gardens... This piece, which brings in many stirring trumpet calls, mingled with a wonderful representation of big guns and rifle fire and a splendidly effective rendering of the national airs of the allies, has been received with much applause whenever it has been played and we learn that on Wednesday the friends of the different hospitals are arranging to

commandeer all the motors they can get to bring the wounded soldiers to the Zoo. These band afternoons are becoming more popular every week.[10]

In September the condolences of the council were sent to Dr O'Carroll, a member of council, on the death of his son who had been killed in the Dardanelles. Mrs Barrington, the manageress of Haughton House, was sent condolences on the death of her husband.

The Easter Rising, 1916

In April 1916, the Zoo was preparing for a good Easter. The hay bill was causing concern but the half-price entry for the entire Easter weekend held the promise

Young visitor with peacock in Dublin Zoo, early twentieth century.

Chimpanzee with
Dr Benjamin B. Ferrar,
superintendent from
1911 to 1938.

Mr McCann, left, and W. Edward Peebles on the ice, February 1912. Peebles was president of the Society in 1916.

of a solid boost to the funds. On Monday 24 April, superintendent Benjamin Ferrar had gone to the Royal Barracks as usual. The Zoo was busy in the morning but as word filtered through about fighting in the city, most people left. A family from Dalkey could not get home and returned to the Zoo to be lodged in Haughton House for the night; they left the next day. Young keepers Jack Supple, J. Flood and Tommy Kelly stayed in the Zoo for the next week or so to help Isabella Ferrar, who took charge as usual in the absence of her husband. Fortunately the restaurant in Haughton House had been stocked up for the Easter period and they rationed all available food, giving restaurant food to those animals that could take it. The main problem was feeding the carnivores as large stocks of meat could not be stored in the Zoo. As bitter fighting continued, Isabella Ferrar and the keepers were faced with the choice of putting down some of the carnivores or using other animals in the collection for meat. In the end they killed an old pony, a donkey, a goat and a few dingoes to feed to the valuable lions.

During the week other keepers risked their lives to call into the Zoo to help out. Benjamin Ferrar was able to reach the Zoo on three occasions by way of Islandbridge or Chapelizod. He brought in small quantities of supplies but left again each time. There

was heavy firing around Phibsborough on Tuesday 25 April, which was audible at the Zoo. On Thursday 27 April, rifle bullets passed over the gardens but there were no injuries, nor were there reports of animals being injured through fright. By Monday 1 May, the fighting in the city had ceased and the military authorities allowed horse meat to be delivered to the Zoo. It arrived just in time to avoid the necessity of having to make further unpleasant choices. Rumours about the Zoo having to shoot the lions and tigers remained untrue.

On Saturday 6 May, nearly two weeks after Easter, six members of council arrived for their scheduled meeting to support Isabella Ferrar. Several members of council including surgeons Sir Charles A.K. Ball, Sir Robert Henry Woods and Dr Joseph O'Carroll had worked long hours in the overcrowded Dublin hospitals during the Rising. Ball managed to attend the meeting on 6 May. On 13 May, Phoenix Park was re-opened to the public, normal activities resumed at the Zoo and 19 members and three guests attended breakfast followed by the council meeting. For the war years this was an unusually high number and was a clear statement that the council members were ready to carry on. Isabella Ferrar was thanked for her courage in looking after the Zoo in such difficult circumstances and was given an engraved silver potato dish to acknowledge her work.

In July 1916 General Sir John Maxwell, the military governor appointed when martial law was imposed in Ireland after the Rising, visited the gardens. George the chimp was let out on the lawn to entertain him by washing dishes that had been left ready in a bucket near the water tap outside the monkey house. On 3 August 1916, Roger Casement was hanged in Pentonville Prison, having been found guilty of high treason for his role in attempting to import guns from Germany for use in the Easter Rising. Casement was a former corresponding member of the Society and had donated numerous South American animals when he had been with the British Colonial Service in Rio de Janeiro.

The Great War continues

Following the Rising, the work of the council focused on keeping the Zoo going in increasingly difficult circumstances. The quality of hay was very poor and hard to get, as were most supplies. In 1917 the Board of Works granted the Society permission to grow potatoes in the Zoo. Stockpiling coke and coal was suggested, as prices in 1917 increased rapidly and there was a danger stocks would run out. The aquarium was closed up because there was insufficient fuel to heat the house and a donation of a pair of pythons had to be refused. In August 1916 some stock arrived from the Toronto Gardens, including a Canadian black bear, two beavers and four tree porcupines. In 1917 the Society agreed to look after two black bear cub mascots belonging to a Canadian battalion until the end of the war.

Every effort was made to encourage wounded, convalescent and invalided soldiers to visit. Handbills were sent to barracks and camps advising soldiers and sailors that they could be admitted to the Zoo on weekdays for threepence. Wives and children of men on active service were still being admitted free. Books of tickets were sent to hospitals. Pensioners in the Royal Hospital were admitted free. The Royal College of Surgeons entertained 400 soldiers for tea in the Zoo and no admission charge was made.

Meanwhile the financial condition of the Zoo was disastrous. Visitor numbers had dropped considerably and many of these were coming in free or at a reduced price. Subscribers resigned and there were few applications for new membership. The president of the Society, Sir Frederick Moore, used his own money to pay for a man to clean the gardens periodically. Two weeks of skating in February 1917 helped matters a little and in 1918 foreign soldiers, who paid half price, boosted gate receipts slightly. Australian soldiers were said to prefer Dublin to London when they were on leave and many visited the Zoo to see the famous lions: Dublin's lions were well known in Melbourne Zoo and Sydney's Taronga Zoo.

Bridge over lake, north west corner of Dublin Zoo, looking from below Haughton House.

In November 1916 a letter of condolence was sent to the Society's vice-president, Robert Woods, whose son had died in action. And in September 1918, just before the end of the war, a similar letter was sent to Cecil Pim, a council member, whose son had also died in action.

End of the war

In spring and summer 1919, Dublin Zoo experienced an astonishing increase in the number of visitors despite the depleted collection of animals and run-down facilities. More than 223,000 came to the Zoo that year, a number exceeded only in 1907 during the Dublin Exhibition in Herbert Park. A programme of reconstruction commenced and remedial works to treat rotting woodwork, collapsing roofs, unsafe doors and other repairs were carried out. Demobilised men, organised by the Department of Labour, cleaned and tidied the grounds. Materials were still difficult to get but a legacy from the late W. Edward Peebles, the Society's president in 1916, was used to fund the most urgent works.

Many of the lions had survived the war and were still producing litters of cubs. After five cubs were sold or exchanged in 1919, there were seven males and seven females remaining in the collection. Empress the gorilla died in May 1917 of a digestive disorder, having lived for three years and four months in the Zoo. The Society claimed that the gorilla's longevity in the Zoo was exceeded only by a gorilla in Breslau which had lived for seven years in captivity.[11] The hoolock gibbon,

Sir Frederick Moore, president of the Society 1917–1921, with guests at the Dublin Zoo fête, 1919.

which was never named, died in October 1918, while Charlie and George, the chimpanzees, lived on until 1920 when both died from colon inflammation and resultant peritonitis.

Zoos around the world were beginning to stock up again. On 16 November 1918, just five days after Armistice Day, the animal dealership Hamlyn contacted Dublin Zoo and asked if it had any young lions for sale or exchange. The council sold some lion cubs; it also honoured its pledge to Antwerp Zoo by presenting Nuala, a Dublin-born three-year-old lion, and agreeing to sell the six-year-old lion, Seamus, a son of Red Hugh.[12] Dublin managed to purchase monkeys, cockatoos, a Brazilian tortoise, a wolf and a chimp, while parakeets, a macaw, an antelope and other animals were donated. An attempt was made to take advantage of the presence of Irish officers abroad to get some interesting animals before the army was disbanded. Officers serving in Egypt were asked for camels and giraffes. However the costs had escalated and, on hearing that a camel which had been £16 before the war was now £50, the council abandoned that request. The Zoo was offered some war trophies and a complete German submarine periscope was received

in 1920 and erected in the loft over the elephant house.[13]

Meanwhile the wives and sisters of council members were organising a series of garden parties for members and fundraising fêtes. In June 1919, they held a very successful five-day-long fête with stalls, games, activities and amusements and raised over £4,000. The goodwill generated by the fête encouraged new annual membership. In April 1920, the volunteer stallholders and helpers – 450 people in all – were invited to the Zoo for a garden party to show them the results of their fundraising. This led to another fête and so began the Ladies' Committee and their fundraising activities, which were to become a prominent feature of the Zoo over the following decades.[14]

Outside the Zoo, Ireland was in conflict as the War of Independence spread, but the only significant impact on the Zoo at this stage was a shortage of coke and coal for heating. A fête was held in June 1920 with a military band entertaining the guests. General Sir Nevil Macready who was the commander-in-chief of defence forces in Ireland, the Chief Secretary for Ireland Sir Hamar Greenwood and nine government officials from Dublin Castle became members of the Zoological Society. Then in November 1920, three weeks before

The foot of Sita the elephant returned to Dublin Zoo in 1922 by members of the Sergeants Mess in the Phoenix Park Depot on the disbandment of the Royal Irish Constabulary.

was ignored), the council became concerned about its annual government grant, which was still £500. On investigation they were assured that until the Southern Irish Parliament came into existence, its grant would be made 'by the imperial parliament or by the crown colony government which may come into existence for the south of Ireland.'[16] At the annual general meeting the council thanked their staff for their loyalty over the past few years. Then they returned to the matters of buying and selling animals and chasing up valuable donations.

In January 1922 the Provisional Government took over from Dublin Castle, and in March 1922 the council received a letter from Constable Major Fitzgerald of the Royal Irish Constabulary saying;

Bloody Sunday, the council decided to postpone the dance it was planning in the Royal College of Surgeons, saying, 'after careful consideration the council feel that under existing circumstances, the holding of a dance by the Society might be misunderstood.'[15]

When the Government of Ireland Act in December 1920 set up the six-county parliament and administration in the North, and a similar provision for the South (which

The RIC sergeants' mess desired to present to the Society the foot of the elephant 'Sita' which was shot in the gardens by a party of RIC on 11 June 1903 after it killed its keeper. The foot had been dressed, mounted and presented by Colonel Sir N. Chamberlain to the sergeants' mess. In view of disbandment, a general meeting of the mess resolved that the foot should be presented to the Royal Zoological Society of Ireland in recognition of past favours towards members of the mess.[17]

Visitor numbers 1896–1922. The peak in 1907 was due to the Dublin Exhibition held in Herbert Park, Donnybrook. Visitor numbers also rose in 1919 following the end of the First World War.

Chapter 4

Peaceful Resort

1922–1950

Summary

The period covered in this chapter was surprisingly good for Dublin Zoo. It should have been an unsettled time with the new political regime, the Great Depression and the Second World War. Yet the records, the newspaper reports, visitor memories and the loyalty of the staff all suggest that Dublin Zoo was a place of 'peaceful resort', as it was described in the Society's 1923 annual report. Visitor numbers remained consistent with an average of 150,000 each year until 1941 when they escalated rapidly to reach 349,000 in 1950. Few 'star' animals were purchased during this period but the lions kept breeding, the bison had calves, tigers and leopards shared the steamy atmosphere of the Roberts House, the chimps entertained, the Children's Corner was created and Sara the elephant gave rides. A dominant feature of this period was the social activity for members and their friends; tickets for parties,

dances, dinners, fêtes and bridge tournaments were so popular that one wit suggested that the Zoo should sell their own tickets on the black market to raise extra funds. While the parties kept the Society afloat, the bulk of the visitors went to the Zoo when entry was cheapest.

The relationship with the new government

The Society's declared loyalty to the British crown since the 1890s and the patronage of King George V did not affect its relationship with the new government. The continuance of the grant of £500 was approved in April 1923 and raised to £750 in 1925. Ernest Blythe, the Minister for Finance, and Patrick Hogan, the Minister for Agriculture joined the Society. And in June 1923 Timothy Healy, the first Governor-General

Clockwise from top: Young visitor with boa constrictor; Scene in Dublin Zoo, c.1934; Kangaroos in Dublin Zoo c.1934.

of the Irish Free State, who had been a member of the Society since 1898, visited the Zoo in a formal capacity. In his address he praised the Society for its work in 'creating an interest in natural history and a love of living creatures'.[1] The atmosphere in the Zoo at Easter 1923 was described in the following newspaper report:

Since 1916 Easter Monday has been a day of public uneasiness. But that is passing away. Never were such crowds seen in the Park as on yesterday afternoon. The Zoo elephant was working overtime. Everything in the Gardens was lovely. Perspiring humanity struggled

Donkey in Dublin Zoo with visitors, c.1934.

bravely for moving space in the lion house. The monkey house was easily first in favour. It was besieged by everybody, old and young. The only dissatisfied visitor was a venerable lady who remarked in a polite whisper, as she endeavoured to force her way to the exit door: 'A little of this goes a long way'. The Zoo was the scene of our only rebellion yesterday. It began when the announcement went for the umpteenth Easter Monday in Dublin's history that the wonderful institution would have to close its doors.[2]

The one noticeable development in the Society's minutes during this period was a new interest in encouraging people from Belfast to visit the Zoo. Prior to this, Belfast, or indeed any city or town other than Dublin, had seldom been mentioned in the records. In 1923, the council contacted the Belfast Naturalists' Field Club to invite membership and for several years took the unusual decision to support the Club's journal through advertising and donation. It also advertised on handbills and posters produced by the Belfast YMCA in connection with their tours to Dublin, and offered

half price entry on production of a return railway ticket to Belfast. These were exceptional arrangements; the council preferred to use its limited advertising budget to put posters at tram and railway stops and only gave discounts to large groups or charities on request. Advertising in Belfast continued until 1936, two years after the opening of Belfast Zoo.

Building the collection between the wars

Throughout the 1920s and 1930s, the Society's friends abroad acquired animals for Dublin Zoo. Sir Geoffrey Archer, governor of Uganda, sent a young lion named Selim Bey in December 1923. Selim Bey sired one litter in 1927 but died shortly after their birth. Mrs J.F. Kenny-Dillon, wife of a bank official in Tanganyika, brought with her several smaller cats and some deer from Africa when she was visiting Ireland in 1925. The same year Mr Shirley V. Cooke, an Irish district commissioner in Kenya, put an advertisement in the local paper in Nairobi asking Irish men to secure animals for Dublin Zoo. He was unsuccessful in getting permission from local Kenyan authorities to send a hippo and a rhino to Dublin but he did send lions

and other cats. He also sent a pair of elands in 1923 but, owing to concern about foot-and-mouth disease in Britain, they remained in quarantine in London for nearly two years. Cooke sent the next batch of animals to Ireland via Antwerp. In 1928 and 1930, Dr A.B. Monks of the Health Department in Sierra Leone sent chimpanzees, monkeys, a baboon, a crocodile, a pelican and a python. In 1929, Captain A.T.A. Ritchie, a game warden in Nairobi, sent baboons, a civet cat,

mongooses, a vulture and others. During the 1930s, Cooke continued to send animals to Dublin Zoo from Africa; in one of his letters, he commented, 'it is a great thing that the council has such a fine institution that Irish-men of every shade of politics and religion can wholeheartedly support.'[3]

Canada and the United States became new sources of animals for Dublin Zoo in the 1920s. Lord O'Shaughnessy, president of the Canadian Pacific Railway, arranged a donation of animals for Dublin Zoo. Rocky Mountain goats and sheep, Canadian black bears, porcupines, and a pair of wapiti arrived in February 1924. The wapiti stag had been in captivity for six weeks and was confined to a wooden crate on the trip across the Atlantic. He looked feeble and shaky when he was let out of the crate but suddenly, with a surge of energy, he jumped the fence of his enclosure and escaped into Phoenix Park where he ran for many miles until he stopped by a small pond near the Castleknock gates. The keepers watched him for a while and decided to leave him there for the

Scenes from water sport competitions held in the Dublin Zoo lake. During the 1920s and 1930s, these events included diving, water polo, pike fishing and, in 1924, the international Aonach Tailteann Games.

night. Next morning, they approached but he ran, jumping over the barbed wire fence surrounding the Magazine Fort and down the hill. He collapsed and a soldier from the Fort stayed with him until the keepers arrived. They tied his legs and brought him back to the Zoo. The animal died later that day. The female wapiti, which came with him, lived on.[4]

The elephants

Sandari, the female Asian elephant, had been unwell for some time and died in 1930. Dangiri Amma and Chanchal Perry, both female Asian elephants, were purchased in 1929 and 1932 respectively. Dangiri Amma was poorly suited for giving rides, which may have been the reason Chanchal Perry was acquired. In 1936 the Governor of Madras presented Saraswathi, a young female who became known to generations of children as Sara. Meanwhile Dangiri Amma was becoming increasingly difficult to manage. In 1938, shortly after Benjamin Ferrar's retirement, she pressed the former superintendent against a wall, breaking several of his ribs. Only James and Jimmy Kenny could control her and there was little chance anyone else could handle her even with training. So in November 1939 the council decided that she must be destroyed.

Making arrangements to shoot Dangiri took several months as the council and the army officer

Clockwise from top left:
Senior elephant keeper
James Kenny, c.1936; Asian
elephant, probably Dangiri
Amma, with Jimmy Kenny
(son of James Kenny)
and young visitor, c.1934;
Elephant, possibly Sara,
arriving at Dublin Zoo. With
keeper James Kenny; Asian
elephants, probably Dangiri
Amma (rear) and Chanchal
Perry, in Albert Tower. c.1934.

Asian elephants, probably Dangiri Amma (rear) and Chanchal Perry, in Dublin Zoo c.1934, with keeper James Kenny looking on.

who was assisting could not agree on where she should be destroyed. The council wanted her shot in her house; the army officer wanted her to walk down to the lake to be shot where the high bank would be a safe background. A compromise was reached and sand bags were brought into the Zoo to create a background near the rabbit rockery. Cedric Flood, who was appointed superintendent in 1938, recommended that Chanchal Perry be destroyed at the same time. Sara was proving to be an excellent elephant for children's rides and Chanchal Perry was surplus. Word about the impending 'execution' of the elephants leaked out. A Mr Dickson of Belfast Coalfields offered to take at least one of the elephants but suitable transport could not be arranged. A letter writer to *The Irish Times* encouraged the public to support Dangiri Amma with donations: 'she is not a very good tempered animal but yet on account of her clever tricks she is a great favourite'. Another wrote;

It is indeed tragic to see this gentle creature blissfully accepting pennies for plates of potatoes from her young admirers, whilst a few yards away the post is ready for her, complete with shooting platform and sandbags.

It was also reported that a woman in Mount Merrion wanted to turn one of the elephants out to graze on half an acre of land at the back of her house, and a little boy in Stillorgan wanted to keep one as a pet. In July 1940, both elephants were shot and no public statement was made. However a report in *The Irish Times* said:

Dangiri Amma is dead! The news, in that form, may not convey anything to anybody, but in simpler terms it means that the large elephant at the Dublin Zoo, that majestic exile who for many a year has been the awe-inspiring joy of every youngster and has

Left: Chimpanzee with Cedric Flood, superintendent from 1938 to 1952. **Right:** Dublin Zoo keepers, 1932. Front row (l-r): Jack Supple, Christopher Flood, James Kenny. Back row (l-r): Charles Flood, Joseph Rice, Tommy Kelly, Christopher Caffrey and Ernest Newsome.

caused even the grown-ups to pause and brood on such immensity, is no longer with us... the death of an elephant is no ordinary event. It is like the removal of an imposing landmark, and the Dublin Zoo will not seem quite the same without Dangiri Amma... Her smile at a bag of buns was almost notorious![5]

James Kenny retired in 1940 and Jimmy Kenny, his son, succeeded him as the elephant keeper. He established a partnership with Sara that was to surprise, delight and provide lasting memories to many Zoo visitors in the mid-twentieth century.

The superintendents

Dr Benjamin Ferrar retired in 1938. He was replaced briefly by Lieutenant Colonel A.G. Doherty and then by Cedric Flood, an engineer who had spent many years managing tea plantations in Assam and Sri Lanka. Flood's genial manner made him popular with members and with regular visitors, whom he encouraged to join the Society. He often walked around the Zoo holding the hand of a chimp and he

was known to turn a blind eye when children slipped into the Zoo over the boundary railings. He developed a very good relationship with the press and vigorously promoted the Zoo, providing photo opportunities and interesting stories. For the first time a superintendent became the face of Dublin Zoo.

Staff relations

The continued popularity of the Zoo during the 1930s ensured that staffing levels were not affected by the Great Depression. Yet their working conditions had barely changed since the nineteenth century. In 1938, Cedric Flood informed the council that some employees had joined a trade union. Within months, staff wages, holidays and leave were examined and wages were increased. All keepers were given a half-day's leave each week and all employees allowed paid annual leave. Random bonus payments continued for successful breeding or at the end of a busy week, and the elephant-keeping staff were allowed to keep the money generated by the sale of buns and vegetables to the public for the elephant. It is also likely that keepers received tips for giving visitors a close encounter with

Memories of visitor, Rowland Eustace

Well-known Irish falconer, Rowland Eustace (b.1926), was a frequent visitor to the Zoo during this period.

As a child I was interested in all animals, birds, spiders. I lived in Rathmines and used to cycle to the Zoo on our half day from school on a Wednesday and on a Saturday – and on any other days when I skived off! I always went in the back gate and parked my bike there. No one paid any attention to me. I used to sit in the lion house and spend hours watching the animals. At feeding time the keeper would come in and wave the meat around to get the lions excited. There was great snarling when they were eating. One of the cats would leave a piece of meat and wait for the rat to appear and then catch that. The lions on the far side of the lake would roar, and then the lions in the house would roar and it was a fantastic sound. They would keep that up for maybe five minutes. I can still smell the aroma of the lion house.

The keepers got to know me and let me pet the leopards through the bars. The leopards would rub their heads against my hands and purr loudly. I was there when there was a lion tamer with a chair and a stick and three young lions. The keeper lifted me up, I must have been quite small, and put me into the cage with the tamer and the little lions. Behind me the mother was banging her paws on the metal sliding door and I was more worried about her than the cubs.

On one occasion in the 1930s I spotted a kestrel sitting in a monkey cage on concrete. It had been donated by a member of the public. I asked a keeper if I could have it; he gave it to me in exchange for 20 mice. I became a falconer, bred kestrels and co-founded a falconry club. In the 1940s and 50s, I remember that there were buffalo heads, rhino heads and other animal trophies all around the walls on the ceiling of Haughton House. And in the 1960s I brought my own children to the Zoo quite regularly when they were young.

Harriett (Daisy) Eustace and her children, Rowland and Hope in Dublin Zoo in August 1930.

Clockwise from top left: Ground floor cafe in Haughton House, opened 1939; Dubliners Joe Dowling (age 5) and his sister Marie with a lion cub, c.1941; Lions with cubs in the Lion Arena, opened 1941. The original wall of this enclosure is now the backdrop for the Play Forest.

an animal, something the council tacitly condoned. In 1940, no pay increase was given but an emergency bonus was paid to help with the rising cost of living due to the outbreak of war.[6]

The Second World War

The animal collection decreased from 1939 onwards as very few animals were available from abroad. In the months after the declaration of war, several British zoos contacted Dublin to see if it would take some of their animals. In most cases, they wanted Dublin Zoo to pay transport costs, which it could not afford. The council was also concerned about the potential cost of feeding some of the larger animals and declined most of them. As the war progressed, Irish people turned to the Zoo in the hope that they could leave their pets there to be fed and cared for. Many budgerigars and parrots were donated or deposited in the Zoo as bird feed became difficult to get. Tortoises, rabbits, goats, geese, badgers, and occasionally lizards, a chameleon, deer and monkeys were also received. A most unusual

Pat McCormac holding lioness Flame, and superintendent Cedric Flood.

donation was brought in by the tenor, Pat McCormac, in 1942. He arrived with a female lion cub called Flame on a lead. The story was that Flame had been born on a stage in Leeds during an air raid and its mother had been killed. McCormac had rescued her and fed her on Cow & Gate baby formula. When Flame was eight months old, he brought her to Ireland, keeping her on the plane with him, then walking her around Dublin city on a lead. Flame became well known in Dublin Zoo and began breeding in October 1945.[7]

As the war continued, the Zoo sought the public's help to deal with animal food shortages. Advertisements were put in the newspapers asking for donations of broccoli leaves, old cabbages, small apples and greens, to which many people responded. Gifts of condensed milk, tinned meat, pears, honey, peas, leeks, cheese, birdseed, white maize and acorns were also presented. Sources of hay fluctuated, as did the price. The supply of wheat stopped in 1941 and, later in the war, bread was strictly rationed. Licences were required for other supplies but the Department of Agriculture said that the Zoo could purchase barley and oats for animal use without a licence.[8] Apple trees were planted in the Zoo to provide fruit for the animals and for use in the tea rooms.

Meat for the carnivores was a constant problem and, in summer 1941, the council announced that they would have to destroy some of their animals if they could not get a supply of horseflesh. Shortly afterwards, the Zoo received permission to shoot a herd of wild goats at the Scalp outside Dublin and the Department of Lands sent carcasses of deer to the Zoo. Donations of donkey, pony, horse and deer meat were received from private donors. Several property owners, including Kathleen Lawless of Newcastle, County Dublin, and Miss Tottenham of Ashford, County Wicklow, allowed the Zoo to kill deer on their properties.

Children's Corner

In 1940, Cedric Flood suggested that the camel house should be turned into a space for tame or domestic animals where children could mix with them without danger. The Children's Corner, later called Pets' Corner, opened the following spring and remained open until autumn. Over the coming summers, Children's Corner was reopened and became very popular despite the fact that there was a separate charge to enter it. The stock changed each season depending on what was available. Lambs, kid goats, rabbits, puppies, tortoises and pigs were often there, as were lion cubs when they were still small enough to be played with safely. Cedric Flood's daughter, Yvonne Ward, and Yvonne's aunt, Peggy Shannon, managed the Children's Corner. The women were given Zoo overalls and permission to wear slacks. A teenage boy helped to keep houses, cages and enclosures clean and tidy.[9]

The Lion Arena

During the early years of the war, Dublin Zoo was supported by government in terms of grants under unemployment schemes to renovate and build enclosures in the Zoo. Work undertaken included an open-air bear enclosure for the smaller bears, a seal pond (for which there were no seals yet), and an open-air lion enclosure called the Lion Arena. The Lion Arena was a significant new development for the Zoo. It was situated on the west side of the lake and used a moat rather than bars to contain the dangerous animals. The concept of using moats for containment had been developed by the famous showman and animal dealer Carl Hagenbeck in Hamburg Zoo in Germany, which opened in 1907. Visitors to Hamburg Zoo could see predator and prey separated only by a moat, and they could watch lions prowling up and down without having to look through metal bars. Hagenbeck's design concepts had spread around the world. In 1939, Dublin Zoo's lion keeper Charles Flood visited the lion enclosure in Edinburgh Zoo and returned with ideas for Dublin. The high wall at the back and sides of the new Lion Arena was made from concrete and granite. A water-filled moat separated the lions' 'stage' from the visitors. Granite was used to hold up the retaining walls and renowned botanist, Robert Lloyd Praeger, a member of council and later president, planted the surrounding area with shrubs.[10]

In August 1941, a pair of lions, Brennus and Noreen, were transferred to the Lion Arena. Brennus had been presented by Bristol Zoo in 1936 and Noreen had arrived from Chester Zoo in 1937. When they moved from the Roberts House to the new exhibit, the council reported that they were 'terrified on finding no obstacle between them and the public, or between them and the open sky'.[11] Brennus was startled by a jackdaw and jumped into the moat and drowned. Imitation railings were placed in the enclosure to help other lions adjust to their new environment. As the lions settled down, the railings were gradually removed. Cairbre and Noreen mated and, in December 1941, Noreen had a female cub. But over the following years, several more lions fell into the moat and in 1952, they were moved and the Lion Arena was converted for use by the polar bears.

The bomb

On 31 May 1941, early in the morning, German bombs were dropped in Dublin, mostly on the North Wall, and 37 people were killed. A bomb fell close to the Dog Pond in the Phoenix Park, 140 metres from the Zoo boundary. Michael Ward, who had been evacuated from England with his mother and brother, was living with his maternal grandfather, Cedric Flood, in Society House. He remembered the night vividly:

> I woke up when I heard the plane and shouted, 'that's a German plane'. I had lived in Heathfield in the South of England, which was known as 'Bomb Alley', before I was evacuated and I could easily identify a

Professor Fitzroy Pyle and Mrs Patricia Pyle, living in Mount Merrion, were family members from 1941. Writer and art critic Hilary Pyle recorded memories of their frequent visits to the Zoo:

To me the Zoo was an experience. The animals, birds and reptiles stay in your mind. Some became friends, like Sara the elephant – the thrill of riding in one of the seats on her broad back, swaying along beside the lake, and wondering would one fall in. She was the only elephant for years, and it was quite a surprise when a little elephant [Komali] became her companion. And the merry smile of Mr Kenny her keeper.

The reptile house was dark and warm with another, older, fatherly keeper. And the surprise when he put a python round my neck. The reptile was warm and dry, and heavy, with strong muscles, instead of being cold and slimy, and it was very much in command despite the keeper's friendly reassurances!

The lion house had strong odours and growls, and one got out rapidly. Bonzo the monkey was lovely. The Children's Corner then seemed very tame, but gentle, with little calves and cuddly things. The Zoo was very pretty.

For me the best part was always when we left the cages and walked to the other side of the lake with open, if still confining areas for deer, lions and a restless polar bear. One day they put some gibbons on an island, and this was the best of all.

Although my parents were members, we seldom went to Haughton House, which was very exclusive, or even to the open restaurant, there wasn't any money, and we brought sandwiches. We took the 43 bus to Donnybrook and boarded the 10 bus to the Phoenix Park. Then a longish walk to the Zoo itself, it seemed longer every time to a young impatient child.

Clockwise from top left: Patricia Pyle with cockatoo 1941; Sara the elephant with Hilary, Fergus and Fionnuala Pyle; On the trap in 1941 (l-r): Hilary, Fergus, Fionnuala and David Pyle; Party in Haughton House, 1945 with Hilary (2nd left) Fionnuala (4th left) David (standing) and Fergus Pyle; Hilary Pyle on a pony; On the trap, middle row, David, Fergus, Hilary with Fionnuala Pyle back right; Bonzo the monkey with Fionnuala, Fergus, Hilary and David Pyle; Hilary's 6th birthday at Zoo in 1942 with Flame, lion cub.

Above: Queuing to get into the Zoo, 1940s. **Left:** Michael Ward, older grandson of superintendent Cedric Flood, in Dublin Zoo in the early 1940s.

German plane. I went to wake my aunt, Peggy Shannon, in another bedroom and was standing beside her bed when the bomb exploded. Every pane of glass was blown out but all of the shutters were closed and they took the glass. No one was injured. The family were up like a shot and ushered down under the stairs. My grandfather took a gun and went outside with Peggy who was holding the torch. He was only worried about the wolves because they're scavengers and would vanish quickly. Lions and leopards would make for the open. But all was in good order. Not a pane of glass was broken in the lion house.

Next day, my grandfather noticed that the bison had charged the railings but not broken through. And Sara the elephant had opened her door, gone down to the lake, and then returned to her house. We found her footprints and noticed that her door was open.[12]

Guests at the strawberry breakfast, 1942, with Lord Holmpatrick (right), president of the Society 1934–1942, and superintendent Cedric Flood (left).

In August, 1941, the council gave the Department of Defence an undertaking that all dangerous animals would be destroyed in case of emergency and cartridges for the rifle were made available.

Social events

The strange feature of Dublin Zoo's experience of the Second World War was the busy social calendar. Following the success of the fêtes organised by the Ladies' Committee in 1919 and 1920, the practice of holding events in the Zoo had taken off. The range and frequency of breakfasts, garden parties, dances and other social activities had increased in the 1930s with garden parties attracting more than 400 people, dances about 800, the members' breakfasts attracting up to 350 people and hundreds attending the bridge tournaments and dinners. From 1932, members of the diplomatic corps in Dublin were given honorary, temporary membership of the Society and their attendance added an air of prestige to the events. Functions usually took place in Haughton House or in a marquee erected on the lawn outside Haughton House. Changing facilities were provided for guests who arrived by bicycle; a tent for the men, while women could change in Haughton

House. Demand for tickets for was such that, by 1944, tickets for the dance were issued to members of the Society only.

When the lake froze in January 1940, skating was possible for five days. Members were allowed in free of charge; their family and friends were charged two shillings and sixpence, and the general public were charged five shillings. The Zoo remained open until 11.00 p.m. each evening with oil flares lighting up the lake and the refreshment room making hot drinks available.

The increasing number of visitors during the war years put great strain on the catering services in Haughton House. By now the entire building was devoted to catering; in 1938, a blind kangaroo, which had been kept on the ground floor of Haughton House, died and the cages were dismantled. The Veranda Café opened there in 1939. In January 1942, Haughton House could still provide tea with hot scones, home-made jams, and assorted pastries. Four-course lunches were also available, which was a considerable feat on the part of the manageress, Ella Murphy, who ran the restaurant from 1940 until 1943. For big occasions, the Zoo used outside catering, often from the Dolphin Hotel of Essex Street, but catered for everyone else

Ice skating in Dublin Zoo, March 1947, with the Lion Arena in the background.

themselves. In February 1942 a notice was put up in the members' room that owing to gas rationing the gas fire would not be lit, but tables near the log-burning fire in the large tearoom would be reserved for them.

Breakfast with the council

In February 1942, a journalist from the *Evening Herald* attended a council breakfast and left wondering how he could become a member of the group. There was a blazing fire in the council room as the men stood and ate 'a bowl of as nicely-cooked porridge as ever I tasted'. The reporter had made the mistake of sitting down to eat his porridge but his host 'murmured in an undertone that it was the custom of the council to take their porridge standing and, slightly embarrassed, I corrected my gaffe'. The porridge was followed by eggs, bacon, sausage and thinly sliced black pudding. At the end of breakfast he withdrew and sat by a fire in another room while the council got on with business.[13]

Sara the elephant

Sara was the star of the Zoo during the war. Under the control of Jimmy Kenny, she gave rides, ate buns, knelt, raised her trunk, lifted her leg, played a mouth organ and stood by patiently as visitors had their photograph taken beside her. In 1941, Sara developed severe problems with her feet and rides had to be discontinued until she recovered. She received a regular pedicure from Jimmy Kenny and grooves were put in the concrete floor of the elephant house in the hope of easing the pressure on her feet but it was not enough. A set of boots was made for her by Wilson of Capel Street with leather uppers and iron soles. According to *The Irish Times*, her boots 'make a noise like that of a weary labourer in hob-nailers crossing a cobbled street'.[14]

However, the boots were expensive, costing £14 a set, and they frayed rapidly on the hard path near the elephant house where she walked up and down with children sitting in the howdah on her back. In 1942, Cedric Flood managed to get five tons of turf mould,

At Zoological Garden Party

Above: The Society council, January 1947. Back row (l-r): G. C. Dockeray, D.B. Gilmore, Brig. Stokes, E. Sheridan, Leslie Bishop, G. Shackleton, Thos Mason, E. T. Murphy (assistant superintendent). Front row (l-r): G. F. Mitchell, J.E. Hogan, A.S. Gordon (president), Jas. Fisher, R. Lloyd Praeger. **Left:** Sara the elephant with keeper Jimmy Kenny.

Post-war

In 1945 a huge party was held in the Zoo to celebrate the end of the war. All staff were given an extra day's pay in anticipation of the crowds expected on 29 June 1945, the day of National Thanksgiving. In May 1945, an acknowledgement was sent to Dr Hempel, formerly German Minister to Ireland, who resigned his honorary membership because his mission had been terminated. In November 1945, the council deferred their discussion as to whether to admit the Czechoslovak consul as an honorary temporary member of the Society until some research had been carried out. They found in his favour and, in 1946, he was among the 1,200 guests at the June garden party. Tickets for the event were in great demand; Hugh Brett, a *Sunday Independent* reporter, described the scene:

which was spread to a depth of several centimetres along 180 metres of path directly beside the lake. This worked well and Sara was ready to give rides again. The elephant rides remained by the lakeside until they officially ended in 1961.

Any husband who wanted to convey bright news to his wife last week had only to tell her that he had two of the coveted tickets. I met a bookmaker who told me he had offered a pony [£25] for four tickets, but there were

Elizabeth Moore

Elizabeth Moore, née O'Dea, in Dublin Zoo, aged four in 1940 (right) and 14 in 1950. Her mother was a life member and the family visited the Zoo frequently from their home in Rathgar. Elizabeth remembers:

Once we got past the thatched entrance, we ran ahead of our mother to the monkey house. On one occasion when I was about five, I was watching the chimps, Charlie and Susie. Charlie was a very big chimp and he was sitting hunched up with his back to the bars. I clearly remember a woman was there, poking him with her umbrella, trying to get him to turn around. Even at five I knew that that wasn't right. Suddenly Charlie whipped around and grabbed her umbrella and slowly ripped off all of the fabric before holding the skeleton of the umbrella over his head.

Outside Haughton House there was an ancient giant tortoise that used to wander on the lawn. I also remember so well the rides we had on Sara, swaying to and fro along the lake. Mr Kenny also let us feed Sara with carrots from battered tin plates. We absolutely loved Mr Kenny; I don't know what it was about him but he was so kind to everyone, treated everyone the same and remembered everyone.

A Zoo photographer took the photo of me on the pony, and my uncle who was visiting from England took the one of me with the reptile. It was outside the reptile house and Mr [Tommy] Kelly was standing by.

68

no takers. If the Zoo people had decided to black market the tickets themselves, he hated to think of the extra monkeys [£500] they might have collected. We had a whale of a time. I enjoyed particularly the two speciality dances, the camel dance, Humps-a-daisy and the Llamabeth [sic] walk... It was novel going round the houses in the Gardens at night-time. 'Any water?' said the parrot. 'Any whiskey?' riposted a sarcastic bystander.[15]

However the end of the war did not mean the end of rationing and the problems with supplies for the restaurant and the animals continued for some time. Eleanor French, manageress of Haughton House, complained that there was no cold storage so meat and ice cream were being wasted, the ice cream wafers were being lost through contamination by mice, the Zoo's sweet and biscuit rations were too small to be of any use, and gas restrictions were hampering her ability to keep a supply of hot scones available. As a result parties had to be limited in size and the 1947 fête had to be cancelled.

The lack of fuel threatened the health of the animals and the council was forced to apply to the Office of Public Works for permission to chop down trees to provide fuel. Lloyd Praeger identified 47 trees that could be felled. As that supply ran out, a further 22 trees were marked for felling but in November 1947, just in time, the council got permission to buy some coal. Around this time the superintendent's house, Haughton House and the switch room were linked to the electricity supply. Electricity was extended to animal houses over the following years.

In 1947 the pressure of making ends meet prompted the council to increase the adults' entrance fee, which had not changed since 1872, from one shilling to one shilling and sixpence. Children remained at sixpence. In 1945 cheap entry on a Sunday had ended and finally in 1947 all remaining cheap entry periods were abolished.[16] A great tradition had ended but the visitors continued to pour into the Zoo.

The fête, dance and other parties resumed in 1948 and were more popular than ever. By now even the members' tickets were rationed, which was causing

Sea lion and keeper, 1947.

New sun cages on the monkey house, 1942.

some annoyance. The Ladies' Committee and the council received a large allowance of tickets each and this may have been what prompted one Society member to write to the council in July 1948 protesting the unfair allocation of dance tickets as she tendered her resignation. A few months later, another member sent in his subscription but said that he was joining only on condition that he would receive tickets for the annual dance.[17]

Post-war: restocking the Zoo

During the years following the end of the war, zoos around the world were attracting greater numbers of visitors than ever before and expeditions were organised to capture wild animals to restock these zoos. Dublin received many offers of animals from abroad but, owing to lack of transport, quarantine restrictions and of course the usual lack of money, the council could purchase only a few animals. In 1947, the first consignment of animals to arrive to Dublin Zoo by air flew into Shannon from New York and included two chimps; the council noted that it was an expensive way to transport animals but that they had arrived in perfect condition.

Sea lions also arrived by air and a sea lion pool was created at the upper end of the lake, transforming this part of the Zoo. After heavy rain the following winter, pike, perch and roach were carried down by flood waters into the pool and were eaten by sea lions. Shortly afterwards, however, the lake began to change colour to a rich brownish red after heavy rain. The source of the contamination was the coal stored in an area of the Phoenix Park some distance from the Zoo. The sea lion pond was affected and the animals stopped eating. They were moved to a small enclosure but it was too late and two of them died. The third did not eat for 54 days but began to recover once it started eating again. There was no question of returning it to the sea lion pond until the coal was removed from the Park or a by-pass around the pond was constructed to control the water inflow. The surviving sea lion was sent to Chester Zoo.[18]

Tuberculosis

Even as animals were arriving from abroad, a serious problem arose with an outbreak of tuberculosis in the monkey house and later in the Roberts House. Several primates had died of the infectious disease in 1923

Visitors in the monkey house, late 1940s.

and again in 1940. After each outbreak all the cages in the monkey house were disinfected and feeding utensils were sterilised. In 1943, a tiger, which the Zoo had received from the Bertram Mills Circus, died of tuberculosis and a lion died of advanced tuberculosis the following year. Any animal in the lion house showing signs of wasting without apparent cause was destroyed.[19]

The chimpanzees and monkeys were among the most popular of the animals. The *Carlow Nationalist* described a typical scene in its 'Dublin Diary':

Saturday afternoon finds us at the Zoo paying our respects to the tenants of the monkey house... The citizens gathered around Charlie's apartment wear the unmistakeable aspect of persons waiting for something to happen. What precisely they are waiting for is not quite clear. At the moment Charlie does not seem to be doing anything besides squatting on the floor of his cage, huge and gross and jolly, like a mediaeval baron recovering from a seven-day binge. Then someone, a small

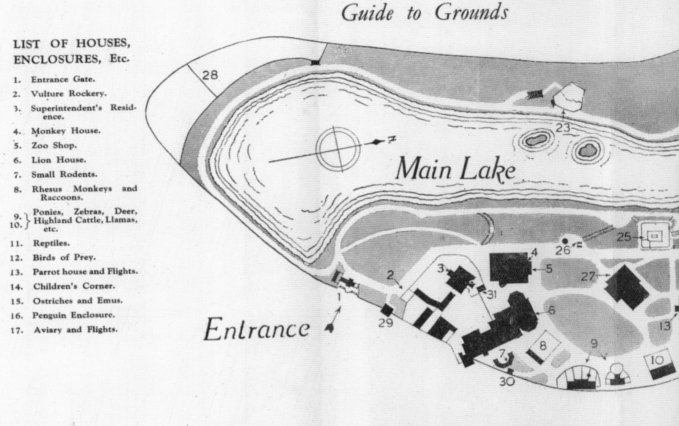

ZOOLOGICAL GARDENS, PHŒNIX PARK, DUBLIN
Guide to Grounds

LIST OF HOUSES,
ENCLOSURES, Etc.

1. Entrance Gate.
2. Vulture Rockery.
3. Superintendent's Residence.
4. Monkey House.
5. Zoo Shop.
6. Lion House.
7. Small Rodents.
8. Rhesus Monkeys and Raccoons.
9. } Ponies, Zebras, Deer,
10. } Highland Cattle, Llamas, etc.
11. Reptiles.
12. Birds of Prey.
13. Parrot house and Flights.
14. Children's Corner.
15. Ostriches and Emus.
16. Penguin Enclosure.
17. Aviary and Flights.

1949 map of the Zoo.

character in a seedy waterproof says, 'Give him a cigarette... We light a cigarette and heave it into the cage. It drops at the feet of Charlie who betrays only the faintest flicker of interest. The small character in the seedy waterproof emphasises the cigarette by poking at it with a stick. His attention thus engaged, Charlie allows a monstrous finger to fall athwart the cigarette which he rolls back and forth until the glowing cinder is barely visible.[20]

In November 1946, the keepers began to suspect that both Charlie and Susie, the other chimp who had been 'taught by the children of Dublin to spit',[21] might be sick. Tuberculosis was prevalent in the Irish population at the time and, because it was an infectious disease, people did not talk about it openly when it affected those close

to them. In the same way, the council was not prepared to refer to tuberculosis in the animals directly; instead it called it an 'outbreak of sickness' caused by poor diet over many years, lack of sunshine during the past summer and the impossibility of maintaining a suitable temperature in the house in the late autumn.

As the disease took hold in the monkey house, glass screens were put outside the chimpanzees' cages to protect them from germs but Charlie died and Susie had to be destroyed. When the Siamang gibbon showed signs of the same illness, the monkey house was closed to the public. In January 1947, two more monkeys were destroyed and others died including a sooty mangabey, which was about 20 years old and was known for turning a somersault after being offered food. Tuberculosis then appeared in the Roberts House where a leopard died of the disease.

A thorough programme to eliminate the infection

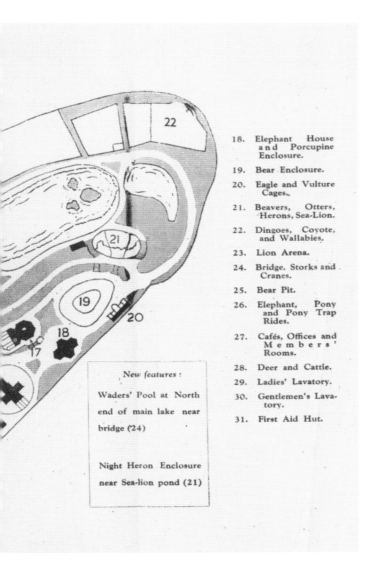

18. Elephant House and Porcupine Enclosure.
19. Bear Enclosure.
20. Eagle and Vulture Cages.
21. Beavers, Otters, Herons, Sea-Lion.
22. Dingoes, Coyote, and Wallabies.
23. Lion Arena.
24. Bridge. Storks and Cranes.
25. Bear Pit.
26. Elephant, Pony and Pony Trap Rides.
27. Cafés, Offices and Members' Rooms.
28. Deer and Cattle.
29. Ladies' Lavatory.
30. Gentlemen's Lavatory.
31. First Aid Hut.

New features :

Waders' Pool at North end of main lake near bridge (24)

Night Heron Enclosure near Sea-lion pond (21)

commenced. Isolation houses were provided for the surviving animals away from the public. Disinfectant was sprayed, cages were scrubbed out with boiling water and washing soap to dissolve grease, then sprayed with hot Lysol or Dettol. Where possible, a blowtorch was turned on bars, doors and all other ironwork in the cages. Arrangements were also made for employees to have their chests x-rayed. By spring 1948, the crisis had passed and the Zoo was ready to restock.

Royal Zoological Society of Ireland

On Easter Monday 1949, the Republic of Ireland was formally inaugurated by Taoiseach John A. Costello and was no longer part of the Commonwealth. In December, Frank Aiken, a senior member of the Fianna Fáil party (then in opposition) asked the Taoiseach whether organisations using the word 'royal' would be asked to

MGM Lion

The Irish lion industry flourished under the management of senior keeper Christopher Flood until his death in 1933. His son Charles succeeded him. Although the market for lion cubs was slowing up, there was still a demand from dealers. The lion cubs were also a very attractive feature of the collection in Dublin Zoo, especially when they were let out in the Children's Corner.

In spring 1947, it was reported in the newspapers that MGM, the American film company, was seeking a new lion for its famous logo and came to Dublin to take photographs of Stephen the lion. Between 1928 and 1958, three lions were used in the MGM logo. There are no records to suggest that Stephen's image was ever used but the belief that a Dublin Zoo lion was the same one featured in MGM's logo spread, probably from the publicity surrounding this visit. It was even suggested in a paper written in 1962 that a male lion Cairbre (1927–1944) was used in the logo but there are no records to support this claim.

However it is possible that Slats, the first MGM lion, was a Dublin Zoo lion. Between 1915 and 1921, 23 male lions were born in Dublin Zoo. Most survived and a number were sold or exchanged with various dealers and zoos, including several in the United States of America. Whether one of the lions born during this period ended up as the MGM lion can only be speculation; there is no record that this was the case in either Dublin Zoo or in the MGM archive.

In July 1949, George Emerson, a famous Hollywood animal expert, asked the council if he could hire 15 lions for the production of the film 'Quo Vadis' in Italy. The council refused, citing quarantine regulations as the reason why they could not agree to the request.[22]

drop that word from their titles before the estimates for the coming financial year were completed. Costello replied that he would not be putting any of them under pressure to do so. At this stage the Royal Zoological Society of Ireland was receiving an annual grant of £1,000. Con Lehane T.D., of Clann na Poblachta was not satisfied:

> Is the Taoiseach aware that the retention of this objectionable anachronism is motivated by a desire on the part of these organisations to parade their hostility to the aspirations of the majority of the people and will the Taoiseach at least make it plain that they

will not be permitted to cock a snook at the people while at the same time accepting a subsidy from them?

To which Costello replied:

> The view I take of this word 'royal' is that it is a historical evolution of our own country... I regard this word 'royal' as a matter of no significance or importance, and not worth wasting time over.[23]

And that was the end of that matter, as far as Dublin Zoo was concerned, for another 45 years.

Visitor numbers from 1923–1949. During the Second World War few animals were acquired yet visitor numbers soared.

Chapter 5

Growth and Decline
1950–1980

Summary

This was a period of fundamental change for zoos, including Dublin Zoo. The traditional approach to buying, selling and displaying animals was coming under scrutiny. Wildlife experts were concerned at the vast numbers of animals being removed from the wild to restock zoos after the Second World War. Public disquiet at animals being kept in cages and small exhibits was being expressed. As social upheavals of the 1960s influenced attitudes, criticism towards zoos grew louder, and Dublin Zoo was not immune.

At the same time zoo professionals began to talk to each other. The old ways were being challenged, specifically the commercial trade in animals, the desire to have as many species in a collection as possible, and the presumption that the mere presence of a species was an educational experience for visitors. Zoo directors formed an international union and met regularly to discuss their profession and the future of zoos. From these meetings four objectives for the good modern zoo emerged: recreation, education, conservation and research.

Dublin Zoo participated in these discussions but it did not have the resources to set new standards in animal accommodation or educational services, the two areas in which other zoos pushed ahead. Instead it carried on as before, using gate receipts, members' subscriptions and the very small government grant to build the collection and encourage membership and visitors. The keepers provided visitors with close encounters with lions, snakes, chimpanzees, monkeys, elephants and other animals, all of which created happy memories for a generation of children and their parents, and encouraged repeat visits. The social activities of the Society were especially lively in the

Clockwise from top: Margaret Reinhardt, on her fourth birthday, with her mother, (second right) in the lion house, 1953; Cheetah with visitor and keeper William Brophy; Hippopotamus Gilbert and keeper Matt Wilson; Tiger cubs Buster and Not-So-Good in Terry Murphy's kitchen.

Bashful (left) and
Happy with a
young visitor.

1950s and 1960s, with summer dinners and dances carrying on into the early hours of the morning.

But even as the Zoo flourished, the changes in attitude towards zoos and the growing concern about wildlife conservation were building momentum and by the end of this period Dublin Zoo was faced with severe challenges.

New arrivals

In 1951 a pair of giraffes arrived. Doc, the male, and Bashful, the female, had been acquired through contacts in Kenya. A new house was built near Children's Corner and high-quality heating installed. Three years later, a young giraffe was born. It died soon afterwards but the staff gained valuable experience and the following year they were able to intervene successfully with the birth of another calf. Bashful mothered the newborn calf, which was named Happy. More calves followed, creating very appealing exhibits and providing stock for sale or exchange. When Doc died in 1960, he had sired nine calves during his nine years in the Zoo.

In 1958, using the money raised from the sale of a young giraffe, Dublin Zoo acquired its first hippopotamus, which arrived just in time for Easter. On Easter Monday, 8,000 visited the Zoo despite poor weather, and the crowds around the hippo,

named Gilbert, were such that a queuing system had to be set up to allow everyone to see him. Gilbert became a great favourite and, in 1962, an eight-year-old female was purchased from Rotterdam Zoo in the hope that they would breed. Named Hilda, she took time to settle down and on several occasions was seen to stand on her hind legs and bite chunks out of the wooden beams four metres above her. But hopes that she might breed with Gilbert came to nothing. Gilbert died in 1974 and Hilda was sold on in 1976. Further animals were acquired and in 1987 the first Dublin Zoo hippopotamus was born to Henri and Linda.

Meanwhile many other species in the Zoo were breeding. In 1958 newborn animals included two Himalayan bears, a Bennett's wallaby, eight lion cubs, a zebra, a penguin, lots of birds and four tiger cubs. The tiger cubs were especially welcome because breeding them had long been the desire of the Zoo team. In 1952, two tiger cubs had been born but did not survive. Another four were born, three died immediately and the fourth died a few weeks later. In 1958, Arja gave birth to four cubs. She rejected them but superintendent Terry Murphy and his wife, Kay, hand-reared them in their home in Society House. Two collie dogs called Flossie and Dolly, who were nursing their own puppies, were brought in to nurse the tiger cubs. Terry Murphy wrote:

The collie puppies and the little tigers got along famously and Flossie and Dolly didn't seem to find anything unusual or odd about nursing a couple of tiger cubs among their own offspring. The experiment went very well, even though our kitchen was overflowing with baby animals.

When it was time to transfer the tiger cubs to their own enclosure, the media were invited to see them. The cubs were so used to human contact that Murphy allowed the journalists to handle them. However, it was believed that one of the journalists had a cat that was suffering from feline enteritis and the infection was passed on to the tiger cubs. Within 48 hours, all four were dead. 'It was one of the saddest moments of my life,' said Terry Murphy in his memoir. A year later, Arja gave birth to three cubs. One died and the other two were hand reared by Terry Murphy. They called the male Buster and the female Not-So-Good, as she was sickly. But both grew strong and the pair became celebrated animals in the Zoo.[1]

Lions

Dublin Zoo continued to breed lions in the 1950s as there was still a market for cubs. Often the lions were mated in winter so that their young cubs would arrive in time for Easter. They were brought out to the Children's Corner, where children could play with them while it was still safe to do so. The red-bricked lion house in the heart of the Zoo was an enormous attraction, especially during feeding time. It had an especially pungent smell that was caused by the lions marking their cramped quarters with urine. Although their cages were washed out frequently, the smell pervaded. In December 1952, on the recommendation of a council member, an Aerovap dispenser that released a perfume was installed in an attempt to sweeten the atmosphere. But the alternative scent had its own potency and another council member complained that the house 'now smells like a perfumery'.[2] The dispenser was abandoned and another generation was allowed to experience the true smell of the lion house.

Watching the lions being fed was a popular event for visitors that continued until the 1970s. Gerry Creighton (senior) started working in the lion house in 1964 as an assistant keeper. His son, Gerry (junior), now Operations Manager of Dublin Zoo, began working in the Zoo officially in 1985 but had been

Lion cub, An Tostal, with eight-year-old Christopher Montgomery, 1953. Christopher, who lived in Inchicore at the time, remembers the day well: 'You could pay to get a photo with a lion cub. I queued up and when it was my turn, the keeper put the lion cub in my arms. It was quite large. The photographer said I knew how to hold a lion! I was thrilled and for years I would talk about how I had a lion in my hands.'

helping his father for many years before that. Drawing on his memories of lion feeding together with his professional knowledge of lion behaviour, he explained the scene:

> The smell of urine in the lion house first thing in the morning was so strong, it would make your eyes weep. When I was a young lad, I would help my father during feeding time by pushing the meat cart for him. The lions would pace: they were so in tune with the keepers that they would react as soon as they sensed them coming; they would rub up against the glass and make a lot of noise. With the cats, the noise, the smell and so many people in

Terry Murphy,
superintendent 1956–1984.

the house, it was a very intense atmosphere.
The cats were in such a confined, sterile space
that they would look at one another through
the bars and their sense of competition for the
meat would prompt them to stalk while they
were waiting and when they got to the meat,
they would demolish it in no time.[3]

A new open-air enclosure was created for the lions
on the west side of the Zoo in 1958. Later on a tiger
enclosure and a cheetah enclosure were placed on the
west side under the charge of Gerry Creighton (senior).
Public feeding of the lions ended in the 1970s and most
of the cats were moved out of the Roberts House by 1979.

Terry Murphy

After a very successful 14 years as superintendent,
Cedric Flood died suddenly at his home in the Zoo in
1952. He was replaced by Cecil Webb, Curator of Birds
and Mammals at London Zoo since 1946. Cecil Webb
had served in World War I and afterwards joined the
staff of London Zoo as a curator and animal collector.
He had travelled widely, gathering birds and animals

for London Zoo. When in Dublin he bred hares, an
especially difficult species to breed. In December
1956 he retired to live in Kenya. He was replaced by
Terry Murphy who had been employed as assistant
superintendent of Dublin Zoo since 1944. Murphy had
proved himself very able; he had managed to get the
rat problem in the Zoo under control, had written the
Official Guide to the Dublin Zoo[4] and in 1956 he had
travelled with council members to the Netherlands,
Belgium and Denmark to make contacts and look at
exhibits. In 1960, now superintendent, he went to Africa
with two members of the council where they covered
nearly 10,000 kilometres and developed connections
with game wardens in the hope of purchasing larger
animals. They made a film of the trip called *Not Ours
To Keep*, which was shown in the Rupert Guinness Hall
in St James's Gate. Demand for tickets was so great that
copies of the film were made for distribution to schools
and other public bodies. In 1964, Murphy appeared
on television several times to talk about wildlife and
the animals in the Zoo. He was a keen filmmaker and
appreciated the value of television in bringing the Zoo
and the animals to public attention. Visitor numbers
surged after each broadcast.

Top: (l-r) Deirdre, Neil, Aisling and Denis by an aviary. Bottom: (l-r) Alice O'Flynn on a bench; Denis, Neil and Aisling on the pony and trap; Denis on a pony; Alice's niece Deirdre (left) with Denis and Neil on elephant Jill.

The O'Flynn family

Alice O'Flynn and her late husband Denis joined the Zoological Society in 1960, three years after they were married.

We became members because it was a place where the children could run around in safety and of course the animals were part of it. We had nine children, the first born in 1958 and the youngest born in 1978, so we came to the Zoo with children over a 30-year period. At first we came on Saturdays about once a month and had lunch upstairs in Haughton House. After lunch I would find a nice seat in the sun and the children would run around and come and go. In later years we came in on Sundays after lunch.

We went to the members' dances and garden parties. These events were part of the Dublin social scene, which included Fitzwilliam week and the RDS Horse Show. They were big occasions and we would all dress up, the men in black tie, the women in new dresses. When life membership was opened, we became life members.

Things changed over the 30 years. In the earlier years, in the 1960s, the children were allowed to feed peanuts to the monkeys; that had stopped by the time the younger children arrived. The chimpanzee tea parties in the 1960s were also great, especially when the animals climbed on chairs or sat in the middle of the table. The older children got rides on the elephant although officially I think they had been stopped by the Zoo. Mr Kenny would tell us to wait until everyone had gone and then he would put the kids on the elephant and walk them around. Getting that close to an elephant was always a treat.

Denis (junior) O'Flynn, eldest son of Alice and Denis O'Flynn:

On Saturdays, Alice would pack us children into the car in Blackrock. Parking outside the Zoo was no issue and we could park near the entrance. Inside the first place we would arrive at was the monkeys and, depending on the weather, they would be in or out. Aisling was the eldest and was deaf. It was different then and people who were deaf were often excluded from many things. But the Zoo was so visual and so tactile, and we were so familiar with it, that Aisling was totally included in the day. With her being deaf, we tended to screech a little more but that didn't matter in the Zoo.

We had games like where we were going to go to next. I remember when it was time for the sea lions to be fed, we would run over to watch them. We had tickets for the Pets' Corner; they were not overly strict and we could often get two or three of us in there with one ticket.

As we became teenagers we stopped going to the Zoo because we had other things to do. But I had a soft spot for the Zoo and later on I brought my kids up from the country to visit it.

Above, left: cousins Grace and Ruth Croxon, and Libby and Elanor McElroy in Dublin Zoo, c.1952; above right: Laura Grehan (née McCrum) in Pets' Corner on her 4th birthday, 1963. She was the youngest of ten children and her eldest sister, Betty, brought her to the Zoo for the occasion.

Funding the Zoo

After a fall-off in visitors in the 1950s due to widespread unemployment and emigration, visitor numbers began to rise steadily from 1960 onwards as new animals arrived and the economy improved. It was around now that the profile of Society membership began to shift. In 1960 there were 3,300 members, many of whom were still participating in the exclusive dances, fêtes and other social events. But it was also evident that families from the growing Dublin suburbs were taking up annual membership simply to bring their children into the Zoo free of further charge. Members were given vouchers for elephant rides, Pets' Corner, and pony or carriage rides, and could buy more vouchers at discounted prices. They could also hold parties upstairs in Haughton House and many children's birthday parties or First Holy Communion celebrations were held there.

Despite the good visitor numbers, the gate receipts were barely enough to keep the Zoo going as prices of food for the animals, development costs and staff wages increased. The government grant was still only £1,000 and there was no sign of any political will to increase it. Spare money was spent on buying more animals and there was little left over for creating modern enclosures. As usual, the council spent a considerable amount of time fundraising. Through the

1950s, 1960s and into the early 1970s, the social events for Society members and their friends continued, attracting thousands of people and generating some funds. The Zoo had a club licence to serve alcohol to members and their guests; it also had a dozen bar extension licences annually that allowed the dances to continue well into the night. Unfortunately the amount of money raised at these events was modest when compared to the cost of new animal enclosures. In 1963 there was a desperate need for a new reptile house. The existing one had been built in 1868 and the roof was collapsing. Terry Murphy visited zoos in Germany and Belgium and came back with a plan for a new reptile house, which was to be located on the west side of the lake near the polar bears and would cost £30,000. Several well-attended events over two years raised only £5,812, so the council had no choice but to repair the old house. The reptile enclosures were updated by using artificial rockwork and tropical plants; the old hard-fuel boiler was replaced by an oil-fired boiler, the roof was reconstructed and the skylights repaired.

The social events encouraged some companies and wealthy business people to help out through sponsorship and animal adoption. Esso adopted a tiger, which related to its contemporary 'Tiger in your tank' campaign. Guinness adopted several animals including the toco toucan and the sea lion, both of

Clockwise from top left: Staff, July 1964. Front row (l-r): Paddy Whelan, Joe Smart, Bob O'Neill. Middle row (l-r): John O'Connor (snr), Tommy Kelly, Michael Clarke, Tommy Conlon, Danny Gannon, head keeper Martin Reid. Back row (l-r): Gerry Creighton (snr), Tommy O'Halloran, Matt Wilson, Charlie Stone; Anthony Byrne (4) (right) with his brother Paul (6) on the ponies in Dublin Zoo, 1962; Ice skating on the lake, 1963; (l-r): Maud Van Haaften, Jay Fleming, Gladys Cotton and Maureen Denham; Dorothy Kilroy (front left), now a council member, on the pony and trap being driven by Tommy Conlon; Brothers Paul (left) and Mark Crowther feeding the hippopotamus, 1965.

Feeding geese near the monkey house, 1964

which featured in its colourful advertising campaigns. Council member Kenneth Besson, who owned the Royal Hibernian Hotel and the Russell Hotel, adopted the giraffe called Doc and Herbert, the lion. Merville Dairy, which was owned by the Craigie family, adopted the rhesus monkey enclosure. Victor Craigie was honorary secretary to the council from 1954 until 1977 when he became president for four years. His sister, Florence, was a member of the Ladies' Committee, and another sister, Irene, ran Pets' Corner. If the sponsorship schemes and the social functions did not raise much money, they raised considerable goodwill, publicity and enthusiasm for the Zoo and contributed to the increase in membership.

The social events, which were often reported in the newspapers, helped to promote the Zoo as a place for private functions. One of the largest of these functions was held in 1958 when 5,000 women from many countries attended the Mothers' Union Garden Party. The scale of the event put the Zoo under great pressure, particularly with regard to toilet facilities. Tom McGrath, an electrician who maintained the Zoo's facilities for many decades, said there were few toilets in the Zoo at the time:

> There was one at the gate, one at the restaurant, one at the back of Pets' Corner and one near the elephant house. I was a member of An Óige and, on my suggestion, we put up a marquee with a trench and plywood with holes.[5]

In March 1955, there had been the suggestion of making the members' toilets in Haughton House available to the general public, but members objected. And in 1956, Bord Fáilte financed new toilet facilities in the Zoo. However, the shortage of adequate facilities for the increasing number of visitors remained unresolved for some years.

Reg Macdonald

Reg Macdonald, who lived in Castleknock, attended many social events in Dublin Zoo in the late 1950s and 1960s. He remembers:

When I was very young, in about 1932, my grandfather and my aunt frequently took me to the Zoo. My grandfather George Clifton was a building contractor and worked in the Zoo from time to time and knew the keepers. I remember the elephant house where the howdah was lifted onto the elephant through a trap door in the ceiling. There was a periscope in the attic of the building. [Keeper] Tommy Kelly used to keep lions' whiskers, peacock feathers and shed snakeskins for us. There were three in the family and we used to rush to be the first to get these gifts from him. We would go into the back of the monkey cages and there was one particular keeper who would open the door and an orangutan would climb onto my grandfather's shoulders and search for raisins which my grandfather kept in his pockets for these occasions.

During the very cold winter in 1946–1947, we skated on the pond. When the thaw started, the snow on the bank melted but the ice lasted for a long period. However there were several feet of clear water between the bank and the ice, so the Zoo put a ladder across to the ice so we could go on skating. The ladders acted as a bridge; we didn't worry about falling in, if you did fall in you'd probably get your picture in the paper!

As an adult I became life member of the Zoo because I kept forgetting to pay my annual subscription. Every Friday I went to the Zoo with friends for lunch upstairs in Haughton House. We'd get a few drinks in the bar, then have lunch. The waitresses had been there for years and they all knew us. The stools in the bar were all covered in zebra skin.

Then there were the dances in June on the long summer evenings, they were magical. Up to 20 of us would go in a party. I lived at one end of the park so I'd go down early and get two tables put together, and do a deal with the bartender for whisky, brandy, bottles of beer, because if you went to the bar during the dance, you'd be standing four deep. It was all based on sale or return, so we got our drink organised. During the evening we could wander around the Zoo to talk to the animals and if you were far enough gone, they would talk back to you! Everyone was beautifully dressed. The dances went on until 4.00 in the morning and the keepers were there all of that time.

If it was a wet night it wasn't great because you couldn't go out and about. But on a nice warm balmy June or July evening, with the moon shining, the stars sparkling, you are mellow after two drinks, you could wander off with your wife; it was romantic. You could go to the elephant house, reptile house, the hippo enclosure or wander around the sea lions. The animals were all out, and the lights were on here and there and there would be a band playing in the marquee.

Dublin Zoo from Society House, 1964.

Clockwise from top left: Boy on the giant tortoise, 1964; African rock python, boa constrictor and Burmese python with Terry Murphy. (right), Tommy Kelly and a young visitor; Olive Eaton, Michael Lawlor, Jane Lawlor and Mervyn Eaton with Haughton House in the background, 1965; John Kenny, a member of the Dublin Zoo maintenance team from 1961–1966.

Chimpanzee tea parties

In 1950 Dublin Zoo began holding chimpanzee tea parties on the lawn. At a specific time young chimpanzees were brought to the lawn near the monkey house. They were young, safe to handle and selected for their docile nature. Under the care of the senior primate keeper, Jack Supple, the chimps sat on high chairs by a high table. They were sometimes dressed in bonnets, frilly dresses or dungarees and T-shirts, and large nappies. Children watched in delight as they tipped the cups upside down, played with their food, threw things at each other and generally behaved in a way that children were not allowed to. Keeper Michael Clarke who worked with the primates said:

At first, the 'party' took place behind a wire fence but then it moved to the lawn and the crowds would sit in a wide circle around the table. The chimps would pick at the fruit and play with the mugs. They were never

Top: Jack Supple introducing a chimpanzee to visitors. Above and opposite, top: Jack Supple and the chimpanzees on the lawn outside Haughton House, c. 1960.

hungry so it was impossible to get them to eat. After a while, the keepers would take the chimpanzees around and allow the children to touch them or have their photograph taken with them. If they were frisky, a collar and chain would be put on them and they would be hooked to a chair but they often hopped down and dragged the chair along.

Some adults were uncomfortable with this performance. 'There were complaints with some people suggesting it was a form of abuse,' said Michael Clarke, 'but the chimps looked forward to it, they wanted to get out'.[6] The routine was so successful that Chipperfield, the British animal dealership, which had a good relationship with Dublin Zoo, offered to rent the chimpanzees and their tea party for six weeks. The council refused: the chimpanzee tea parties were a big attraction that encouraged people to visit the Zoo repeatedly.[7]

The difficulty with the chimpanzee tea parties was that the animals could only be used for these events when they were young and safe to have around children. As soon as they grew too big, they were confined to their enclosures where they often lived out their lives in isolation. Nevertheless the council decided that, rather than breed chimpanzees, they would maintain a stock of young chimpanzees for the tea parties and put them on the market when they could no longer be used for that purpose.

Meanwhile superintendent Terry Murphy suggested that an outdoor exhibit should be created for the chimpanzees in the hope that the healthier environment

Margaret Reinhardt on her 4th birthday, May 1953, with her mother, Carmel (in black coat). From Coolock, Margaret was an only child. Her father had died two years earlier of tuberculosis. With very little money for treats, a visit to the Zoo was a special occasion for Margaret and she was dressed in her best clothes.

Chimpanzee exhibit, which was formerly the bear pit. A cluster of flamingos can be seen on the lake to the right.

might encourage them to breed. In 1965, the 1830s bear pit on the slope below Haughton House was remodelled, the wall on the lakeside removed and a moat constructed. This was to be the new home for the chimpanzees. Roses were planted around the top and front of the enclosure and an electric fence was installed. The plan was successful and the first chimpanzee to be born in Dublin Zoo arrived in May 1974. By then the tea parties had come to an end because it had become impossible to find a zoo that was prepared to take on a mature, hand-reared chimpanzee. In 1983 when the Zoo was facing a financial crisis, a council member suggested starting up the tea parties again but the notion was quickly dismissed as not being good for the animals' welfare.

The elephants

The most exciting event for most children visiting the Zoo during this period was a ride on an elephant. Olwyn Lanigan's father was a life member in the 1950s.

He brought his family on regular visits to the Zoo. Olwyn rode on Sara down by the lake:

> I remember the crude howdah; it had a seat on either side and a metal chain across the seat where three children sat. The child at either end could hold onto a metal bar on the arm of the seat but the child in the middle only had the chain to hold on to and I remember it was loose enough and I was small enough to slide underneath it. The steady walk down the lake was fine with the elephant swaying but the turnaround was quite terrifying. During the turn there seemed to be a shift in the balance and as a small child I felt that if the angle was any greater, I could slip under the chain. I held on to the metal bars hard.

Jimmy Kenny was very well known to visitors of all ages and had a knack of creating moments that provided lasting memories. For eight or nine years, Ann Stevens (née Edwards) went to the Zoo nearly every Saturday morning with her father, Richard, specifically to see Sara:

> We lived in the Liberties and I was an only child. My dad worked all week and Saturday was our day. He would take me to see Sara. When she saw me coming down the path, she would recognise me and trumpet a greeting. We got to know Mr Kenny very well and he would let me into her compound. When she gave rides, I sat mahout style on her head and not in the saddle that was used to give the rides. Sara was so gentle; I'd often bring carrots and things to feed her. I cried for weeks when she died.

Ann Murphy remembers,

> Jimmy Kenny made it feel that the ride on the elephant was a fun thing to do and I had no fear; he was great, a lovable sort of man who knew how to talk to children. The elephant

was the pinnacle of the visit; once you'd had your ride, it didn't matter whether you got on the train or the pony and trap after that.

Dorothy Kilroy, now a council member, remembers visits to the Zoo in the 1950s:

> I came here frequently as a child and all I wanted to do was go down to the elephants and feed them bits of potato from battered tins. I used to hang around at the time when the elephant was going down to do the rides in the afternoon. Mr Kenny would select a few kids and put them on Sara, who knelt down so we could get on. Then she stood up. Sitting up front by myself was scary and exciting. I remember the sensations, the rocking from side to side, and going down steps, it was highly dangerous.

Patty de Courcey's parents visited Dublin Zoo on their honeymoon:

Elephant keeper Jimmy Kenny and young visitors on Sara, 1955.

Clockwise from top left: Sara the elephant with Charlie and May (née Halligan) de Courcey, August 1951; Annie and Tom McCormack with their four youngest sons, from left Ollie (10), Johnny (7), Billy (8) and Eddie (4), summer 1954; Connie Kenny, wife of Jimmy Kenny, with son, broadcaster Pat and daughter, Anne-Marie; Sara with Ann Stevens on her 11th birthday in 1959; Asian elephant, Jill, who arrived in 1964, with Maeve and Robert McDonald in April 1966. Robert, aged eight, had just come out of hospital after three and a half years where he was recovering from a serious injury. The siblings were given a week off school to celebrate and the visit to the Zoo was a highlight. Hearing the story, Jimmy Kenny brought Jill out to the lawn for this photograph.

Left: Paul Kenny, son of Jimmy Kenny, on Komali: 'I was nervous during this photo because the bears were in the enclosure right behind me!'. **Right:** Sara after her fall, July 1958.

My parents Charlie and May got married in Waterford on 4 August 1951 at 10.00 in the morning and, after the traditional breakfast, the small wedding party walked them to the station for the train to Dublin. During their three-day honeymoon in the city, they visited Dublin Zoo where Jimmy Kenny arranged this photograph. They had a wonderful honeymoon and I've loved this photograph all of my life; I couldn't believe that my father got that close to an elephant.

Ollie McCormack lived in Galway, and coming to Dublin in the 1950s was a summer treat:

At the time we did not take a summer holiday so a day trip, especially to Dublin Zoo, was special. We left our home early in the morning and travelled to Dublin by train and got the number 10 bus to the Zoo. I remember standing on Sara's leg and it was a very exciting moment; before then the largest animal I had been close to was my dog, Rory.

Paul Kenny, eldest son of Jimmy Kenny, described the popularity of his father:

Everyone knew him, from high court judges to kids. It used to take us at least 45 minutes to get down Grafton Street with my father. If anyone said 'hello', he'd stop for a chat. Many

of the people who came to the Zoo were regulars and he'd remember them all. If they had a camera, he would pose them beside Sara and Komali and take their photograph.

Bob Mooney was Jimmy Kenny's assistant. Paul Kenny said:

Sara played with Bob. She would walk down by the lake in the usual way with Bob and the children on her back. When it came to turn at the lake, she would start backing into the lake. Bob worked out that she was doing it deliberately, and also knew that she would continue to do it regardless of what he said. So he would tease the kids and, when it came to turning around, he would say, 'now, Sara, back into the lake!'[8]

In July 1958, Sara fell while carrying a full load of children. She had been having trouble with her feet for some time and it was believed that she had tripped over a protruding stone on the elephant walk, fallen onto her front knees, and then over on to her side. The children remained in their seats, secured by the chain, apparently uninjured. There had already been discussions about the safety of giving elephant rides; a letter from London Zoo was received saying 'all zoos are considerably worried about the attendant risk and are seriously considering giving up these rides'.[9] Despite her fall and continuing problems with her feet,

Above: Sara and Komali with Gertrude Eustace and her children, Bryan (3), Jennifer (5) and Eric (2), c.1961. **Right:** Komali with Laurie Breen (née Keyes) and her sister Anne, of Capel Street, c. 1955.

Sara continued to give rides until 1961. She was put down in 1962 after all attempts to cure her foot failed. Officially elephant rides were at an end.

Komali the elephant

A young elephant arrived at Dublin Zoo from Ceylon in 1950. Named Komali, she had been found abandoned and had been brought to Ceylon Zoo in the back of a car. She was put into the charge of Jimmy Kenny, who allowed visitors to feed her carrots or bread from a tin plate. In 1958, after Sara's fall, Komali was still not ready to take a howdah on her back. However Jimmy Kenny often allowed children to sit on her and go for a short ride. Olwyn Lanigan remembers a ride on Komali: 'Mr Kenny told me he had to be careful how he put the grey blanket on her back to avoid ruffling her hair because that would be uncomfortable for her'.[10]

From the beginning it was clear that Komali's temperament was uncertain. A month after she arrived, a ten-year-old child had her arm broken when she was trying to feed her. Jimmy Kenny had total control over her but the council was concerned that in his absence

other keepers might not be able to manage her. Their fears were realised one day in May 1963. Jimmy Kenny was on sick leave. The superintendent, Terry Murphy, described the scene:

A busy day for the elephants, c.1964.

[Komali] became agitated and the assistant keeper found he could not control her by his voice alone and, using sheer force, she managed to break away from him and out into the grounds. Close by, a group of school children were enjoying a visit to the Zoo. They were being led by a nun. As they turned at the sound of Komali's trumpeting the nun rushed forward to stand in front of the children. Komali moved past them at some speed, nudging the nun as she went by and knocking the poor lady to the ground. She was not hurt but, understandably, rather shaken.[11]

Jimmy Kenny was sent for. As they waited for his arrival, Komali spotted a tractor nearby. She rushed towards it and the driver managed to jump free before she pushed it over with her head. No one was hurt. Jimmy Kenny

arrived shortly afterwards and took control, leading her calmly back to her stall. Later that year, keeper John O'Connor (senior) was giving her a bucket of water to drink from when she reached out with her trunk and pulled him towards the railings of the stall. His arm went in between the bars and Komali butted her head against his arm. Alterations were made to the elephant house and outdoor area to restrict public access to both Komali and Jill, the elephant that had arrived in 1964. The public still tried to feed them, and at least one elephant fell into the moat around their enclosure while reaching out to take food from a visitor.

There were occasional exceptions to the rule about riding the elephant. In 1967, the actor Tony Tormey was on one of his periodic visits to the Zoo with his parents. At the same time a television crew was recording Ireland's Eurovision entrant Sean Dunphy singing 'If I Could Choose'. Dunphy was sitting on the

Black rhinoceros Laura with calf Ringo, 1969.

back of Jill, by then the only elephant in the collection. Tony recalls:

> The crew saw me and put me up on the elephant with Sean Dunphy – possibly because I had white-blond hair. I was about four. Then Sean Dunphy, who was sitting behind me, started singing that love song in my ear and I bawled my eyes out, it was all so strange. I had always wanted to touch an elephant and I can clearly remember the grey blanket on his back and the feel of the elephant's skin, it was not as tough as I thought it would be.[12]

Over the next 20 years, numerous Asian elephants and a few African elephants were purchased or borrowed; some died, some were sold on or given in exchange. Without the opportunity to ride them, feed them or interact with them, none became as well known as Sara or Komali, who was put down in 1966. Jimmy Kenny retired in 1976 after 43 years of service. In a most unusual gesture, he was invited to the meeting of council so they could thank him for giving so much pleasure to the Dublin Zoo visitors over the decades.

Bim, the elephant seal, being fed by Zoo maintenance man, Tom McGrath, in a picture specially posed for *The Irish Times*.

More arrivals

The buying and selling of wild animals continued unabated in the 1960s with dealers' lists arriving every day. Pam McDonough, a secretary in Dublin Zoo, said: 'Huge numbers of animals were being caught and offered to zoos; it was very tempting but of course we did not have the money for them'.[13] Nevertheless the Zoo did manage to acquire a few of the more popular species, which contributed to the noticeable climb in visitor figures during this decade. In 1960, an African black rhinoceros arrived from East Africa and was called Congo. It was still very young when it arrived and had to be bottle fed. It died of the cold in 1962. That same year a female black rhinoceros was purchased

Above: (l-r) Audrey, Majella, Tony and Valerie Fergus on the wishing chair, c.1974. The family of eight lived in Dundalk. Majella remembers: 'Our Dad worked for CIÉ so we got free travel on the train to Amiens Street and the bus to the Zoo. We would spend the whole day there, walking around, having a picnic, riding on the ponies. **Left:** (l-r) Kevin Breen, Mark Kane, Jimmy Fortune and Alison Breen, c.1977. Kevin and Mark often cycled six kilometres to the Zoo after school to see the big cats. They got to know keepers Charlie Stone and Frank Burke, who gave them the latest news from behind the scenes. In 1978, when three Siberian tiger cubs were born, Kevin and Mark were allowed to see them before they were introduced to the public.

from Rotterdam Zoo and a year later a male was purchased from Bristol Zoo. Both animals were zoo-bred. A new enclosure was built for them on the west side of the lake near the entrance.

In 1969, the female rhinoceros became pregnant. In anticipation of the birth, a special maternity stall was constructed to allow her complete seclusion. Staff monitored the birth through closed-circuit TV and, on 9 July, a male calf was born. Within a few hours, he suckled on his mother. But soon afterwards the keepers noticed the mother becoming agitated and could see no sign of the calf. They quickly made their way to the enclosure and discovered that the calf had squeezed himself through the bars of the maternity stall gate and wandered down the service passage towards the father who was trying to attack him through the bars. The calf was carried back to his mother, who became very aggressive and charged the stall gate. The calf was pushed back through the bars and she quietened down. Ringo, as the calf was named, was sold two years later to a British zoo. In 1976, the Zoo switched to the white rhinoceros species. The black rhinoceros is now critically endangered.

Other arrivals included a southern elephant seal, a species that was acquired by numerous zoos in the 1960s. The enormous animal ate 75-80 lb of herrings a day, costing roughly £1,400 a year to feed him. Fortunately Bord Iascaigh Mhara, the national fisheries agency, agreed to sponsor him and the elephant seal was given the name Bim. A section of the sea lion pond was cordoned off for him. When he became too large for this enclosure, he was moved to what is now the penguin enclosure. He had a habit of flopping his head and shoulders on top of his 1.5 metre iron railings but the staff did not think he would have the energy or initiative to get over the top. One day he was seen waddling along a side road in the gardens; it was late in the day and there were few visitors around. The keepers got a tarpaulin, lured him on to it by offering him some fish, and dragged him back to his enclosure. He was still quite young then. In 1966, Bim escaped again but by now he was a five-metre, two-ton animal. The keepers enticed him into the nearby giraffe enclosure where they manoeuvred him into his original crate and eventually got him back into his own enclosure. An additional fence was placed on top to prevent further escapes. Bim died in 1969; this surprised the council as elephant seals in captivity were known to live up to 40 years of age. The post mortem revealed he had a disease causing atrophy of his heart muscles, which had developed into a fibrosis.

Meanwhile two young orangutans had arrived in 1966 from Singapore with the help of the Orangutan Recovery Service in Malaysia. The Zoo already had Adam, who had arrived in 1958, and they hoped that the young female from Singapore, called Eve, would breed with him. A new ape house was built on the west side of the lake with a dry moat to protect them from the peanuts and other food still being fed to the apes by the public. The orangutans were transferred there in 1971.

Developing international relations

Dublin Zoo's animal collection grew in size and diversity during the 1960s. In 1956, there were 442 animals in the Zoo; in 1968, there were 1,057. Successful breeding and improved animal husbandry accounted for a portion of the increase but the easy availability of most species on the open market was also a factor. Too often young animals were taken from the wild because they were easier to transport, and an adult protecting them may have been killed during their capture. In the 1960s, zoo professionals began to talk in earnest about their responsibility towards animal conservation and habitat preservation and the role they might play in public education.

Nineteenth century zoos had generally worked in isolation from each other. In 1928 the first attempt to draw zoo managers together to work for their mutual benefit was made in Germany, which led to the establishment of the International Union of Directors of Zoological Gardens (IUDZG) in 1935. Progress was interrupted by the Second World War, and in 1946, the director of Rotterdam Zoo started it up again. The establishment of the professional body marked the beginning of the international approach to define what constituted a good zoo, and to provide strategies to help zoos all over the world achieve improvements and be relevant in the growing need to protect and nurture wildlife. Dublin Zoo was first represented at these meetings in 1950 when Cedric Flood, superintendent of Dublin Zoo, attended.

Over the following decades, a complex network of local and international organisations developed to bring zoos and others working with wild animals together. Their common purpose was to conserve species and preserve natural habitats. Their most powerful tool at the time was to establish global studbooks and gain some control over the acquisition of animals

Left: Cedric Flood's badge from the 1951 meeting of the International Union of Directors of Zoological Gardens.

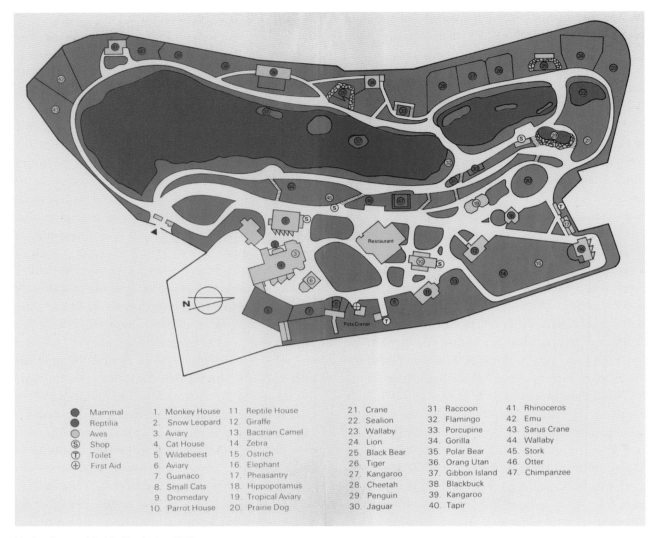

● Mammal	1. Monkey House	11. Reptile House	21. Crane	31. Raccoon	41. Rhinoceros
● Reptilia	2. Snow Leopard	12. Giraffe	22. Sealion	32. Flamingo	42. Emu
○ Aves	3. Aviary	13. Bactrian Camel	23. Wallaby	33. Porcupine	43. Sarus Crane
Ⓢ Shop	4. Cat House	14. Zebra	24. Lion	34. Gorilla	44. Wallaby
Ⓣ Toilet	5. Wildebeest	15. Ostrich	25. Black Bear	35. Polar Bear	45. Stork
⊕ First Aid	6. Aviary	16. Elephant	26. Tiger	36. Orang Utan	46. Otter
	7. Guanaco	17. Pheasantry	27. Kangaroo	37. Gibbon Island	47. Chimpanzee
	8. Small Cats	18. Hippopotamus	28. Cheetah	38. Blackbuck	
	9. Dromedary	19. Tropical Aviary	29. Penguin	39. Kangaroo	
	10. Parrot House	20. Prairie Dog	30. Jaguar	40. Tapir	

Undated map of Dublin Zoo in the 1970s.

and later the breeding of animals in zoos. In 1967 the directors' union reached an agreement prohibiting members from participating in any form of trade in several threatened species including orangutans and Galapagos tortoises. The purpose was to prevent trafficking in these animals. The agreement also demonstrated how the IUDZG planned to have a real impact in the fight to save endangered species. From now on, these animals would be allocated to zoos depending on their facilities and the possibility that they might breed. Of course, a zoo could purchase an animal from a dealer and continue to breed without reference to the central studbook, but such zoos would then find it hard to do business with members of the union.

In 1966 the title of superintendent of Dublin Zoo was changed to 'director' to fit in with the international community. Later that year, Terry Murphy attended the inaugural meeting of another networking group, the Federation of Zoological Gardens of Great Britain

and Ireland (now known as BIAZA). The federation was formed to create a network throughout Ireland and Britain to exchange information, discuss new research and developments in animal husbandry and diet, and create standards for all zoos within the group.

Education

Arising from the international cooperation of zoo directors and professionals, four objectives for a good modern zoo emerged: recreation, education, conservation and research. Of these, recreation was looking after itself and conservation and research were still elusive concepts. Education, on the other hand, was one they were all familiar with; it had been a founding objective for many zoos including Dublin Zoo. Now the zoo directors recognised that merely seeing an animal close up was no longer an adequate response to the educational role of zoos in the mid-twentieth century. However there were no standards or guidelines to follow so each zoo had to create its own programmes. Zoos with resources hired teachers, created atmospheric classrooms, trained tour guides and volunteers, and developed programmes for a range of ages. A few of these reported on their work in the *International Zoo Yearbook*, which commenced in 1959.

But for zoos without resources, such as Dublin Zoo, very little was done during this period. In the late 1950s and 1960s, several council members ran occasional educational programmes for members' children, but it was on a very small scale. The real potential for a solid educational programme was with the thousands of children who came to the Zoo with their teachers each week in late spring and early summer. The Zoo had a deal with CIÉ, the state transport company, to bring busloads of children from all over the country to the Zoo. It was supposed to be an educational visit but it was left to the teachers of each group to direct the children's interest on their day out. By 1980, Dublin Zoo still had no one individual dedicated to developing the Zoo's educational role and it was left to members of the council to fill in the gap as best they could.

150th anniversary celebrations, 1980

As the Royal Zoological Society of Ireland approached its 150th anniversary, the Zoo was in difficulty. The council was still taking an active role in the day-to-day running of the Zoo and they struggled to keep up with the changing economics of the time. Between 1961 and 1966, the annual wage bill alone doubled from £20,000 to £40,000. By 1980, still largely reliant on entrance fees for income, there were severe financial challenges on the horizon. There were also great challenges facing the Zoo with regard to animal accommodation; the small enclosures of the past were no longer acceptable, but with no resources there was little that the council could do.

Celebrations to mark the 150th anniversary of the Zoological Society were held in 1980. A week of parties

President Hillery at the unveiling of the plaque marking the 150th anniversary of the Zoological Society of Ireland in May 1980. Several ceremonies, parties and dances were held in early summer 1980 to celebrate this great achievement.

started on 10 May, the date of the first meeting in the Rotunda in 1830. President Hillery attended breakfast, following which he presented the Zoo with an elephant, which had been a gift from the President of Tanzania. He also unveiled a bronze statue of a squirrel by sculptor Colm Brennan. The highlight of the week was the promenade night party at which guests wore costumes modelled on nineteenth-century clothes design.

While the party was a celebration of 150 years of achievement, it also marked the end of an era. In terms of world-class zoos, Dublin Zoo in 1980 had become an anachronism. The animal collection was too large for the space and most of the animals were being kept in enclosures that had not kept pace with the best international design standards. Staff and visitors were expressing disquiet at conditions in which the animals were living. The four objectives of the modern zoo – recreation, education, conservation and research – were seldom mentioned in the official records. Dublin Zoo was in danger of losing respect at a local and an international level and the forthcoming period was going to test it to the limit.

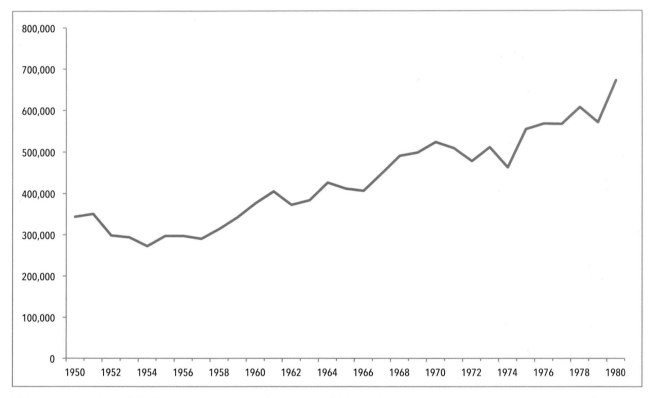

Visitor numbers 1950–1980. The peak in 1980 was due to the publicity and events celebrating the 150th anniversary of the Royal Zoological Society of Ireland.

Chapter 6

Radical Change
1980–2000

Summary

This was the most difficult period in Dublin Zoo's history. The Zoo had fallen so far behind contemporary zoo development that in 1990 it was in danger of closing down. The animal accommodation was inadequate, public facilities were run down and there was industrial unrest among the staff. Visitor numbers fell and even keen supporters of the Zoo despaired. In addition, there was little indication that Dublin Zoo was working towards integrating the international zoo guiding objectives of education, conservation and research into its operations. Still largely reliant on good gate receipts, there was no hope of improving the situation without significant financial help. Nevertheless staff commitment remained high, the council of the Society ploughed on in the face of mounting debts, Fota Wildlife Park was opened, and events were organised including the visit of giant pandas from China in 1986.

Then just before the gates were permanently closed, rescue came from the government, helped considerably by Bertie Ahern T.D., a lifelong supporter of Dublin Zoo. And after a turbulent 20 years, the Zoo could enter the new century with justifiable optimism.

The day out

In the 1980s Dublin Zoo's breeding programmes continued to be very successful and this undoubtedly contributed to annual visitor numbers of well over 600,000 between 1980 and 1982. In 1980, newborns included a chimp, a flamingo, lemurs, a gibbon and a giraffe. The following year, the Siberian tiger, the lion, jaguar, leopard and clouded leopard all bred. And in 1982, three American black bears, two giraffes, a Bactrian camel and a zebra were born. By now many of the opportunities to interact with animals, which had provided previous generations with magical moments, were no longer permitted. Close encounters depended on a chance meeting with a keeper who was prepared to allow the visitor to touch or feed an animal. These visitors included Mike Murphy who was recording a piece for his high-profile television programme, *The Live Mike*. Murphy's encounter with a hippo in 1982 was described in the *Evening Herald* by John Feeney:

> Mike Murphy has landed in a hospital clinic. He was doing one of his home movies in the Zoo. The plan was to persuade passers-by that Murphy was a new keeper who had a special feel for hippos: in fact he could talk to them. With the RTÉ camera cunningly hidden in the prairie dog compound, Murphy had high jinks until he told a woman that he was going for a ride on the hippo. Up got Murphy on the broad and scaly back of the zoo animal but the seemingly sleepy animal was having none of it. It shook and flounced until Murphy was thrown, breaking a finger and severely straining another and his wrist.[1]

Social events for Society members and their friends had dwindled but they still had exclusive access to the upper-floor restaurant in Haughton House. The restaurant was a well-known place for business lunches in the mid-1980s despite being described by one restaurant critic as resembling 'a middling hotel in a provincial town [with] authentic touches like the whiff of Brussels sprouts that hits one at the door'.[2] In May 1985, a new fast-food restaurant for the general public and a lakeside coffee shop were opened by Campbell Catering. A reporter in the *Evening Herald* noted,

It's all a far cry from the old Royal Zoological Society of Ireland when sedate garden parties and private dining rooms made a clear division between those who belonged to the Society and those who just paid their admission fee at the gate.[3]

Animal acquisitions

In the early 1980s, the global zoo community's new approach to animal conservation was beginning to have an impact on the availability of animals. More species were being drawn into international breeding programmes and the transfer of animals from one zoo to another for breeding purposes was becoming more frequent. Records, studbooks and procedures to manage such loans were being developed, making it easier to identify animals that would contribute to the diversity of the species in zoos.

In 1981, Dublin Zoo received an 11-year-old orangutan called Annie from Brookfield Zoo in Chicago on a breeding loan. At the time Dublin Zoo had two male orangutans: Adam, who had been in the Zoo since 1958, and Tommy, who had been there since 1967. The intention was that Annie and Adam would start a conservation breeding group and their offspring would be moved in time to wherever the studbook keeper suggested. However they did not mate and they were both moved on to other zoos. Tommy died in 1983. Sibu, a male Bornean orangutan, and Leonie, a three-year-old female, arrived from Rotterdam Zoo in 1984. They did not mate for many years but according to Gerry Creighton (senior), 'This situation changed when another male, Benji, arrived in 1994. Now there was competition.' Sibu and Leonie's daughter, Riona,

Girl walking towards the monkey house, 1980.

was born in February 1996 and Dublin Zoo's successful orangutan breeding group was established.

The Siberian (now known as Amur) tiger was another species that Dublin Zoo hoped to establish as a conservation breeding group. The Siberian tiger was considered endangered and had been part of an international studbook since 1966. In Dublin Zoo the tigers had been living in an outdoor enclosure on the west side of the lake since 1972 and had bred in 1978. However, in February 1982, before they could become part of an international plan, tragedy struck when one of the Siberian tigers died of tuberculosis. All of the other Siberian tigers, two adults and three young, had to be destroyed. A post mortem on the male Siberian tiger indicated that he had died of tuberculosis of a bovine type. As a precautionary measure the lions in the adjacent enclosure were also put down; there were no tests available for checking whether the lions had the disease while they were alive. It emerged that the

tigers were infected but the lions were not. Quarantine procedures were stepped up and the outbreak was successfully contained.[4]

The international zoo community came forward with offers of replacement tigers and lions and after a six-week period, during which the paddock and dens were treated, two lions arrived. A pair of Siberian tigers was also acquired, one donated and one lent from British zoos. In 1983, much to the joy of the keepers, four Siberian tiger cubs were born. Keeper in charge of the cats, Gerry Creighton (senior), said:

> The loss of our tigers and lions in 1982 was devastating; I had to put them into the back of the van to send them up to Abbotstown, it was the worst moment of my zoo life. Then we bred these four cubs a year later. They were the first tigers to be born after we lost all our tigers, that was why they were so special.

Members of council, May 1980. Back row (l-r): R.J. Dennis, P. Wilson, L.B. O'Moore, D.W. Jeffrey, A. Brady, A. Ganly, J. McCullough, M. Russell, P.N. Meenan, D. McConnell, B. Blennerhassett. Front row (l-r): E.J. Clarke, M. Maguire, M. Taylor, A.E.J. Went, E. Lamb, N.J. Hogan, J. Bigger, J. Carroll, J.S. East, V. Craigie (president), A.G. Mason, P. O'Nuallain, J. Adam, G. Burrows, E.D. Weavers.

The Amur tiger mother tends to be a great mother, and the male Amur, though the largest in the world, is the gentleman of the cats. Now we were back on track and we got a great response, it was very exciting.[5]

Horticulture

In 1981, horticulturalist Stephen Butler, who had trained in Kew Gardens in London, was appointed to the position of head gardener and over the following 37 years radically transformed the appearance of Dublin Zoo. On his arrival the Zoo was, he remembered:

> a very bare and barren place and the animals were always visible. The lake edges were bare and muddy and the geese constantly grazed on whatever vegetation was there.

The Society still prided itself on its colourful beds of roses, tulips and other seasonal flowers but horticulture in zoos had changed and these floral displays belonged to a different era. Modernising zoos were using plants, grasses, shrubs and bushes to immerse their visitors into a world suggestive of wild animal habitats. Butler

was aware of these shifts in zoo horticulture but in the early 1980s his team had to spend a lot of time removing ice cream wrappers and crisp bags from rose bushes after a busy weekend, and mowing the very many small patches of grass around the Zoo. They also had to manage the damage caused by free-ranging geese that ate the grass but left the weeds, roosted on the water's edge, and left their droppings on the paths. Slowly, taking on a small patch at a time, Stephen Butler and his team began the transformation. He recalls:

> There was no question of spending money on mass planting so we propagated almost everything in our small nursery from cuttings and seed. Over several years we planted the lake edges with about 5,000 native Wood Sedge (*Carex pendula*) and New Zealand Satin Flower (*Libertia grandiflora*), both of which could resist the major problem of the geese. Many small labour-intensive grass areas were also removed and replaced with low-growing ground cover such as *Cotoneaster rotundifolia*. This helped reduce time spent on mowing.[6]

The Zoo continued to buy free-ranging geese during

Clockwise from top: Bactrian camels and the electric train sponsored by Bisto that ran from the lawn outside Haughton House. Photograph taken c.1989; Jaguar cubs with Frank Burke; Giraffes, Grainne and Sebastian, with calf. c.1988.

the 1980s and they did not just upset the horticulture staff. Leah Benson described her encounter with the geese as a child:

> We were on a day out in the Zoo with our school. A friend, Emma, and I were near the Pets' Corner eating crisps, which I remember was a really big deal for us at the time. We were left behind by the group and were surrounded by geese. We were about seven years old and about the same height as the geese. The geese were vicious; they didn't bite but they were spitting at us. They wanted our crisps but I remember clearly that we didn't relinquish them! We were completely surrounded for what seemed like an age until someone noticed and rescued us.

The geese gradually died out; they seldom bred and on occasion suffered from instances of mink predation. Eventually the only free-ranging fowl were a few peacocks, peahens and some guinea fowl.

Above: Hippos Linda (left) and Henri with keeper Joe Byrne and his daughter Martina (age 10).
Left: A balcony of the members' restaurant in Haughton House, mid-1980s.

Opposite page top: Keeper Gerry Creighton (junior) with Alma, the male Siberian Tiger lent by the Chipperfield Organisation in England after the loss of the tigers following the outbreak of tuberculosis.
Bottom: Lemurs in c.1990 with Pets' Corner and wishing chair in the background.

Fota Wildlife Park, Cork

The lack of space for the collection of more than 1,000 animals in Dublin Zoo had been a concern for the council since the late 1960s. Repeated requests over many years to the Office of Public Works for extra land in Phoenix Park had so far been unsuccessful and rather than delay any longer the council considered opening a wildlife park. Urban zoos around the world had taken the approach of splitting their collections between an urban site and a rural site with reasonable success. Generally the two sites were managed by one authority that coordinated the animals across both facilities. This encouraged breeding, allowed for larger groups of animals to be kept, and provided visitors with the option of seeing the animals in a natural-looking environment such as open grassland with several species in one exhibit, or close up in the traditional zoo space. Pursuing this model, the Dublin Zoo council looked at sites in Wicklow and Kildare. Then in 1979, Tom Raftery, Professor of Agriculture in University College Cork, proposed that the Society use 70 acres of university land on Fota Island for the wildlife park. The proposal was accepted and plans commenced.

With no government support forthcoming for this enormous undertaking, fundraising in Dublin and Cork was launched early in 1980 as part of the 180th anniversary celebrations. The 70 acres on Fota Island were ideal with 30 acres of parkland as well as woodland, grassland, a slight hill and a lake. It was heavily overgrown but a team led by Sean O'Donovan, University College Cork Farms Manager, was on hand to clear it. Terry Murphy with his animal care

assistant, zoologist Sean McKeown, oversaw the early developments in Fota Wildlife Park. In 1982 McKeown was seconded to develop the park with Tom Raftery and the Cork team, and was appointed the first park manager in 1983. Carmel Conroy, secretary to Terry Murphy, went to Fota in February 1983 to assist with the development.

Giraffe, zebra and cheetah were among the first species to be kept in Fota. The intention was that they would breed and become self-sustaining. Their exhibits were spacious, their night quarters discreet and the barriers that contained the animals unobtrusive. Free-range animals including lemurs and kangaroos were later introduced. In July 1983, the Wildlife Park was opened to the public by President Hillery who described it as 'a most admirable and inspired idea'. For three years, the council had put a tremendous effort into developing Fota Wildlife Park and their efforts had paid off. While there was great enthusiasm for the Park in Cork, few Society members contributed donations.[7] It is likely that Fota was too far away for Society members, most of whom lived in the greater Dublin area, to consider it in practical terms as an extension of Dublin Zoo. It also provided little relief to the crowded conditions in the Zoo.

Strife

While the council were focusing on Fota Wildlife Park, Dublin Zoo was heading into serious financial trouble. Dublin Zoo's overdraft of £37,000 in 1980 jumped to £146,000 in 1982. While revenue from admission and membership grew at a modest rate, costs were rising at a greater rate. The Zoo received a government grant of £5,000 and a Dublin Corporation grant of £5,000, which together only paid for clothing for the staff and the water rates. There were no resources to make extensive improvements in animal accommodation

or visitor facilities and as conditions deteriorated general admissions started to fall. The situation facing the council was compounded by growing staff unrest. In 1983 the council went into negotiation with the Federated Workers' Union of Ireland for a wage increase. In May 1983, George Burrows, a journalist and vice-president of the Royal Zoological Society of Ireland wrote frankly about the serious nature of the Zoo's financial situation in *The Irish Times*:

> The Society is, of course, caught up today in negotiations for the next pay round and it is inevitable that if union demands are to be conceded at any point above the Government's guidelines, the future of the Zoo certainly will be put in jeopardy. There is no other way to get money. It was put to Zoo members on Saturday that if the gate receipts cannot generate enough funds to keep going then some sections might have to be closed off, leading to wage and other savings which in turn would lead to some staff lay-offs or redundancies.[8]

A week later, Brendan Price, a keeper at the Zoo, responded in a lengthy letter, which was also printed in *The Irish Times*:

Keeper Brendan Price at the annual general meeting of the Royal Zoological Society of Ireland, January 1985.

George Burrows, as a writer for your paper and as a one-time vice-president of the Zoo Council, should have known better than to write of possible 'lay-offs or redundancies'. To the staff and their dependants, this was the first indication that any such moves were under consideration... I will not bore your readership with internal politics except to say these are hard times and there is much room for greater efficiencies, but they are not hopeless times. If your paper wishes to report further on Dublin Zoo, I'd welcome more thorough, in-depth investigation of the problems of a management structure, which is 'more old than venerable'.[9]

The exchange opened the way for more public letters and comments about the financial and industrial difficulties of the Zoo. On 9 October 1983, the Zoo was closed for a one-day strike.[10]

Visitor figures in 1984 were disastrous as a prolonged bus strike and the visit of the United States president, Ronald Reagan, over the normally busy Whit Sunday weekend made access to the Zoo very difficult. By the end of the summer, the council was anticipating an accumulated deficit of £260,000 and had no way to pay it other than an unlikely surge in visitor numbers or their traditional method of a special appeal to members. To compound the council's difficulties, several newspapers reported that some staff members objected to the appointment of Peter Wilson, who had been selected to succeed Terry Murphy as director in October 1984. In November the *Sunday Independent* reported:

Dublin Zoo is in a state of crisis. Part of the problem is financial, but not the most serious part. The crisis exists primarily because the animal keepers there are no longer prepared to be seen and not heard. Since they found voice, a virtual state of war has existed between them and those who run the zoo, members of the Royal Zoological Society of Ireland, the inheritors of the Zoo and its charter from Queen Victoria... Part of the staff belief is that because of lack of long-term planning the Society's aim to preserve rare and exotic animals and the requirement on it to provide an educational service are being defaulted on.[11]

Hippos Henri (right) and Linda with director Peter Wilson.

Arrival of the giant pandas, June 1986, with Gerry Creighton (front left) carrying the crate.

Peter Wilson, director

In September 1983, Terry Murphy announced his intention to retire after 40 years of service during which he had steered Dublin Zoo's animal collection through a significant expansion in the 1950s and 1960s, and overseen the creation of Fota Wildlife Park. He remained on until his successor, Peter Wilson, was appointed. Wilson, veterinary surgeon, academic, a member of the Royal Zoological Society council since 1972 and Honorary Secretary since 1977, took up the position of director on 1 October 1984. He had a long association with Dublin Zoo. His father had been a member and he had visited the Zoo regularly as a child. His uncle, Arthur Ganly, was a member of council, and his father-in-law, George Burrows, became a council member in 1973. Other academics from Trinity College had been invited to join the council around the same time in an attempt to bring some younger members onto the managing authority.[12]

Peter Wilson approached the job as director with vigour and in February 1985, Gemma Hussey, Minister for Education, announced a government grant-in-aid of £250,000. This cleared all debt up to the end of October 1984 but without substantial capital funding from the government, which was not a likely prospect given the depressed economic condition of Ireland in the mid-1980s, it could not solve the fundamental problems faced by the Zoo. Public criticism about the running of the Zoo continued and visitor figures remained low until the visit of two giant pandas gave the Zoo a useful boost.

The giant pandas

In June 1986 two giant pandas, Ming Ming and Ping Ping arrived in Dublin Zoo with their keepers on a goodwill visit from China. This was the first time this species had been seen in Ireland. The Chinese authorities controlled the availability of giant pandas so few zoos outside China kept these animals. In the 1980s, the Chinese government surprised the international zoo community when it agreed to lend pairs of giant pandas to zoos in America, Australia and Europe.[13] The animals with their distinctive shape, markings and playfulness made them a huge attraction wherever they went. The giant panda is also the ubiquitous symbol for the World Wildlife Fund. Zoos, including Dublin, used the high-profile visit as an opportunity to spread information about the dangers facing animals in the wild.

In Dublin the arrival of Ming Ming and Ping Ping was an occasion for celebration in bleak times as the country was deep in economic gloom with rising unemployment, emigration and divisive debates about social issues. The

Zoo received sponsorship to help towards the cost of the visit, and the enthusiasm of the media gave the Zoo all the publicity it needed. The giant pandas remained in Dublin Zoo for 100 days and it was estimated that over 350,000 people saw them, which contributed to much improved gate receipts for that year.

The pony and trap

In 1987 the pony-and-trap ride, one of the last of the old Zoo entertainments, came to an end. The pony-and-trap ride was still very popular in the 1980s but in early summer 1987, there was an accident in which the driver, Helen Clarke, and two children were injured. Helen, the daughter of keeper Michael Clarke, had started helping in Pets' Corner in 1973 at the age of nine. She was known for having a natural ability with horses and began driving the pony and trap at the age of 13. She described the incident:

> After I had been working weekends through the summer in the Zoo as a teenager, I left to work as a riding instructor for five years and came back in 1987. Taffey and Stoney were the two ponies that were used for the pony and trap rides and they were rock solid, strong and steady. But Taffey was knocked down and killed over winter. And it was difficult to get a pony to match Stoney. A pair called Rainbow and Festival was brought in that had already been trained. A supporter of the Zoo had bid for Festival in a charity auction against Charlie Haughey and had given him to the Zoo in exchange for a life membership. Festival was easily spooked and was afraid of balloons. Rainbow bit people.
>
> On the day of the accident, they had been going all morning and I was bringing them in at lunchtime. The normal route for the ride was to swing around in a small circle by the old parrot house but the director Peter Wilson was giving a lecture to veterinary students about the snow leopards so I had to go back around the restaurant [Haughton House]. A C&C lorry was making a delivery to the restaurant; the rattling bottles spooked the ponies and they careered out of control. I gave them rein but there was no place to turn. It was May and there were children everywhere and I tried to steer them safely into the yard

Michael Clarke, keeper from 1949 to 1993 and his daughter, Helen Clarke Bennett, keeper and later team leader, African Plains, photographed in 2009.

> where they would have stopped. Two children were knocked down. I saw a building in front and turned them just in time but they hit a car. I was standing – the driver always stood on the trap – and I fell off and ended up under the car. I was in hospital for a week. There were no more pony rides after that.[14]

Education

Just before the arrival of the giant pandas, Dublin Zoo appointed its first education officer, Dr Elizabeth Sides, a marine biologist with a keen interest in public education. Her appointment was funded by the Zoo after the council realised that they could no longer hope for government support to employ a professional educator. There was only money for a salary and, without resources or support, Elizabeth Sides was given a room and left to get on with it. Undaunted she made connections with primary school teachers to develop ways of enhancing their students' visits to the Zoo. She produced worksheets and teacher supports, created sets of slides and gathered biofacts. Hands-on activities were organised for the children:

> We did all sorts of creative things on a shoestring. To teach kids about the bats, I made templates and, using those, the kids cut out bats from coloured paper. We hung their creations on branches. The simple nature of the materials did not detract from the children's enjoyment one bit. They were busy, having fun and learning.

In 1988, Elizabeth visited zoos in Toronto, Boston, Chicago, San Diego and others in North America. The

Above: Young African Elephants Judy (left) and Debbie. Council member Margaret Sinanan (at rear) is conducting a group of children on a tour of the Zoo. **Left:** Elizabeth Sides at the launch of periodic newsletter, Zoo News, late 1980s.

teaching experience. Teaching materials were also prepared for special exhibitions such as the visit of the golden monkeys in 1987 and the koalas in 1988. Her last big job before she moved on was to prepare educational material for the well-attended Dino Live exhibition in 1993.

The volunteers

Shortly after taking up her educational role in the Zoo, Elizabeth Sides was asked to establish a volunteer programme. The idea of having a well-trained body of people who could assist with groups or be on hand to provide snippets of information to visitors about the animals in an informal way had become common in zoos around the world. Given the sheer volume of visitors to urban zoos, especially during busy times, the supporters, known variously as 'volunteers', 'docents' or 'friends', contributed to the educational objectives of a zoo while remaining aware that visitors wanted a relaxing day out. Elizabeth Sides invited Society members to join the new volunteer programme in 1987. The response was reassuring and about 100 people commenced a rigorous training programme designed, scripted and delivered by Sides. The course continued

tour, at her own expense, gave her ideas, especially about signage. On her return, she redid all of the signs in the Zoo but again she was limited in what she could achieve:

> I would love to have had the resources to design the graphics in a different way, with diagrams of animals' behaviour that could tell you quite a lot about what is going on. But there was no money for illustrations so I did a lot of those myself.

Elizabeth also toured Ireland and spoke to primary school teachers about the educational possibilities of the Zoo. She delivered classes to some students, and provided worksheets and teacher notes to the many others who could not be accommodated with a direct

From top to bottom: New signage created by Elizabeth Sides, 1989; Keeper Brian Stone at the chimpanzee enclosure addressing visitors; The volunteers' Discovery Cabin near the sea lion pond, 1995;

for 12 weeks and many dropped away; some thought that they would get contact with the animals, others saw it as a revitalisation of the social side of the Royal Zoological Society, but Maeve McDonald, an original volunteer, remembered:

> The training course was very comprehensive with a lot of scientific terminology and we had to study and concentrate. But it was very interesting and drew me in. As a test, Elizabeth took us out in smaller groups to listen to us speak about the animals and make sure we were not making up our answers to questions.

After the first group of volunteers graduated, Sides worked with them to explore ways in which they could be useful around the Zoo. Mary Neville, another of the first volunteers, said;

> We were to go down to the gate and offer people tours but the public didn't like that, they thought we were going to charge them. The following season we stood by enclosures with a large badge saying 'Ask Me'. We were asked some very bizarre questions.

The volunteer programme took off with a new group graduating each year. Some were available during the week, others at the weekend with the volunteers helping Elizabeth Sides with the rosters. An old cabin was made available and placed near the sea lions. Surrounded by the small but growing collection of animal teeth, bones and other biofacts, usually cleaned by Sides, volunteers based in the Discovery Cabin answered questions and encouraged visitors to explore what was there.

As the volunteers experimented with ways of enhancing visitors' experiences in the Zoo, the Zoo staff were also working out their relationship with the volunteers. The volunteers had arrived at a time of great uncertainty so they had to work hard to show that they had something to offer. A move from the Discovery Cabin to a section of the Roberts House near the lawn gave them a boost. Visitors could see that there was a welcoming space with something inside to interest children and they ventured in. Maeve McDonald said: 'When we moved there everything improved. It was a great location and very easy to attract people. We were able to put up information displays and lay out the biofacts'. As time

went on, they convinced the keepers that they were there to help and were not going to take over anyone's job.

Continuing crisis

Although the volunteers added a layer of support to the work of Dublin Zoo, the financial crisis was getting steadily deeper. The excitement and extra income generated by the visit of the giant pandas in 1986 quickly vanished and once more the Zoo's management found itself having to deal with poor quality animal accommodation and tatty visitor facilities. Even people who were supporters were despondent. Eileen Cooper ran a kindergarten and brought the children to the Zoo on their annual visit:

> The animals weren't injured and the staff were doing their best but the animals simply did not have enough room. The polar bears were the most upsetting. But I knew that it was only by supporting the Zoo that things could improve.

The two polar bears, Spunky and Ootec, were the focus of many visitors' dismay. The pair had come to the Zoo in 1980 from Churchill, Canada, where they had been caught on a rubbish dump. They were very popular with the public but as they matured, signs of their repetitive behaviour bothered many visitors. In 1989 an RTÉ television investigative programme, *Today Tonight*, showed the polar bears walking up and down and made references to their 'psychotic behaviour'.[15] Margaret Sinanan, who joined the council in 1981, said that being a member of council in the 1980s was difficult at times. 'There was a lot of anti-zoo feeling about and I felt defensive; all I could say was that we understood and were trying to do something about it, but we simply did not have any money to do it.'

In 1988 a grant of £250,000 from the National Lottery fund kept the Zoo going for a short while but when it became clear that the Zoo could not support itself, the government established a working party to investigate. It was led by Mick Doyle, a veterinary surgeon and former Irish rugby coach. But even as Doyle's investigations got underway, the Zoo continued to sink rapidly. Gate receipts were the lowest since 1974, business in the restaurant had fallen by nearly 75 per cent, the long tradition of providing the council with a cooked breakfast prior to meetings was dropped to save money, and the strawberry breakfast for 1 July 1989

Above: Polar bears Spunky and Ootec in the former Lion Arena on the west side of the lake. Left: Minister for Labour, Bertie Ahern T.D. with president of the Society, John D. Cooke, at the opening of the Bat House, October 1988.

was cancelled because of a postal strike. Yet another grant, this time from the Department of Education, made sure that animals were fed and staff were paid, but by now a debt of £320,000 was forecast and it was stated at a council meeting that 'legally speaking the responsibility for the entire deficit fell upon members of the council personally'. The Taoiseach, Charles Haughey, visited the Zoo, but only said that he would

wait for Mick Doyle's report. When pushed, he said that he was 'slightly tired of these panic statements from zoological quarters'.[16]

Bertie Ahern, however, was taking a keen interest in the fate of the Zoo. He was the local member of Dáil Éireann and a frequent visitor to the Zoo. Born in 1951, he had spent most weekends as a child in or around the Zoo. His father managed the farm at All Hallows College and he often walked with him through Drumcondra to the Phoenix Park. If his father was not available to take him to the Zoo, Bertie Ahern and his sister, Eileen, would make their own way and walk around the perimeter looking at the animals. 'You could see quite a lot then,' he said. Bertie Ahern continued to visit the Zoo as a young adult and then as a parent:

In the '70s, I watched the Zoo go downhill. There was no money around and very little change, just the odd bit of paint and some wire, but they were incidental changes. Then in the 1980s, the condition of the Zoo got worse and, as I wheeled the girls around the Zoo, their prams would get stuck in the potholes in the paths.[17]

Bertie Ahern first intervened in Dublin Zoo's troubles in 1987 when he was Minister for Labour. With 19 per cent unemployment in Ireland at the time, he was responsible for overseeing a FÁS scheme called the Community Youth Training Programme (CYTP). Under this scheme, experienced tradesmen and apprentices were employed to work on selected projects that would last for between six and 12 months. As a charitable organisation the Zoo qualified for help from this scheme. Dan Mahony, a construction supervisor with FÁS who started working in the Zoo in July 1987, said:

> We began with the old bird aviary. The walls were decaying, crumbling, and we demolished most of it, leaving only some small base walls. We stripped the inside and effectively built a new house.[18]

This building became the Bat House with bird aviaries on the outside. Rodrigues fruit bats and the smaller Seba fruit bat were acquired and signs carrying a conservation message were displayed. The Bat House was opened by Bertie Ahern in October 1988. Theoretically, the FÁS team was supposed to move on to a new location but Bertie Ahern arranged it so they could remain at the Zoo. They began work on transforming the monkey house into the South America house using plans designed by architect David Keane, a member of council. The building was gutted, leaving only the bare structure but then the work was halted; while the government had provided the labour, the Zoo was responsible for the materials and the money had run out.[19]

Facing closure

In December 1989 it emerged that Dublin Zoo had only enough money to pay staff wages for two more weeks. For the first time since the rocky foundation years, the

Zoo football team 1991–1992. Back row (l-r): Noel Duffy, Anthony Ward, Willie Phillips, Joe Byrne, Phil, Paul Stone. Front row (l-r): Eddie O'Brien, Kevin O'Moore, Jim Quinn, Peter Phillips, John O'Rourke.

council began to investigate the notion of closing the Zoo permanently. The Zoo limped on through the lean winter months but in March 1990, the decision was made to close the Zoo after St Patrick's weekend if sufficient funds were not forthcoming. Team leader Eddie O'Brien remembers the reaction of staff to that news:

> Peter Wilson called a staff meeting and said that funds weren't going well and there was likely to be no money for wages. The staff got together. We made stickers saying, 'save our zoo', and used all of our contacts to get help. We got supplies of food for the animals for nothing. The Save the Zoo Pound Appeal was launched. A guy with a tape of a song called 'Save Dublin Zoo' was here every weekend with a bucket collecting money. Visitors came to support us and to see the Zoo for the last time. Around St Patrick's Day, the Zoo was very busy.

Fundraising campaigns received widespread support from schools, banks, shops, small companies, the ESB and many others who raised money. Their encouragement gave moral support to the Society and the staff and helped to counter the continuing negative publicity. The Zoo survived the summer but in September, the council considered closing once more; the idea of going through another winter without help was too daunting. The autumn and winter were miserable. Wolves had to be put down because of a disease outbreak, a raccoon killed one of the Chilean flamingos, and there was negative publicity around the death of a polar bear cub and the euthanasia of the African elephant, Judy. Even the food at the candlelight dinner at Christmas, one of the few social events left for members, was judged to be poor.

Rescue

But Bertie Ahern was keeping abreast of developments. The Doyle Report was completed in July 1990 and given to Ahern. He was now Minister for Finance, and in December 1990 a supplementary estimate of £670,000 was made for Dublin Zoo through the Department of Education. It was enough to pay off debts and allow work by the FÁS team on the South America house to recommence. The new house was opened on St Stephen's Day in 1991 by Bertie Ahern. The FÁS team then moved on to work on the reptile house. Curator of reptiles Gerard Visser from Rotterdam Zoo helped

Pebbles, a hand-reared lemur, with keeper Charlie Stone.

DUBLIN ZOO – AN ILLUSTRATED HISTORY

Chimpanzee, Sunny, with keeper Eddie O'Brien.

with the design and the collection, which concentrated on East African reptiles. Facilities to promote breeding were incorporated into the design.

Although the work of FÁS was encouraging, the problems that had brought Dublin Zoo to the low point remained. The debts had been paid off but fundamental changes to what was still a nineteenth century institution were urgently required. Public affection for the Zoo would not be enough to save it from further debt. The Doyle Report was thorough in its analysis and took into account the latest international thinking about the interlinking objectives of recreation, education, conservation and research. It assessed each exhibit in the Zoo, recommending that half of them required major modification and the polar bear exhibit should be closed if extensive improvements were not carried out immediately. The Doyle Report also stated:

> The role of Dublin Zoo is perceived as that of the national zoo of Ireland. It appears to us to have been pure folly for the Royal Zoological Society of Ireland to have persisted with the word 'Royal' in its title and not to have amended the name of the Society. We hope that this small matter can be put right for it must be damaging the image of the Zoo for those from whom it should expect help and support.[20]

The council were open to the recommendations for reform. During 1993, the word 'Royal' was dropped from the name of the Society, a new constitution that reflected modern business structures was devised, and two senior civil servants were co-opted onto the council. Then, in November 1993 a £15 million development plan was approved by the government.[21] Seán Cromien, who retired as secretary general of the Department of Finance in 1994, and Barry Murphy, chairman of the Office of Public Works, joined the council. In 1995 John Barry, a human resources consultant, helped to negotiate what became known as the Dixon Room Agreement between management

Director, Peter Wilson, with president of the Society, David McConnell, and Minister for Finance, Bertie Ahern at the 'Dino Live' exhibition, 1993.

and staff. The agreement was an essential element in the steps taken to ensure the continued financial survival of the Zoo and allowed for redundancies and early retirement. It also restructured the working week, reorganised the teams based on location within the Zoo, promoted training with Sparsholt College in England, and introduced a new career path for staff.

The redevelopment

With the level of capital funds available to introduce some of the best international habitat design concepts, the first task was to fix some of the poor infrastructure in Dublin Zoo. Martin Heffernan, an architect with the Office of Public Works, led the redevelopment team. The installation of a ring sewer around the Zoo took priority. Up until then, the enclosures for the rhinoceros, llamas, blackbuck, orangutans, lions and others on the west side were drained into the lake. The ring sewer caused great disruption but was essential. In the circumstances however it was hardly surprising that visitor figures dropped to 387,000 in 1995, the lowest number since 1962.

Once the sewer was in place, Martin Heffernan and the redevelopment team had an opportunity to introduce new habitats that supported the four objectives of a good modern zoo. They visited zoos abroad to find out what worked and what did not. The result in Dublin Zoo was a mixture of themed areas based either on the classification of the animals or on geography. The architects wanted to give the animals some privacy so features were incorporated to allow animals to get away from public viewing areas if they wished. They also wanted to give visitors a chance to experience the animals close up with an element of surprise. Thick glass walls featured in many of the enclosures in the hope that the visitor might have a face-to-face encounter with a wild animal. The Zoo team provided technical information, particularly about aspects of containment.[22]

The list of enclosures that were completed between 1996 and 1998 was remarkable. The World of Primates was ready in July 1996. In 1997, Bertie Ahern opened the second phase of the City Farm, which had replaced Pets' Corner, and the first phase of Fringes of the Arctic, which included accommodation for bears, arctic foxes and snowy owls. In 1998, he opened the World of Cats and the jaguars, lions and snow leopards were moved into these more spacious areas.

For the first time in Dublin Zoo, horticulture was

included in the design. External landscapers were used for the World of Primates but the Zoo's own horticultural team did all of the landscaping for the World of Cats and Fringes of the Arctic. Stephen Butler said:

> Although there were disagreements as to how much money was available for plant purchase, we eventually spent ten times the original offer, and the effect was immediate. It was our first planting of bamboo, an expensive choice, but very quick to fill in. There was some themed planting with all South American plants near the jaguars, mainly Himalayan plants near the snow leopards, and a jungle appearance from the bamboo and tall grasses for the Sumatran tigers. The Arctic Fringes were easier, we just used very bland non-showy plants with small flowers and small leaves, such as the birch and cotoneaster.[23]

Other exhibits completed in the Zoo in 1998 included the tapir exhibit and the penguin exhibit while another phase of the City Farm and the wolf exhibit neared completion.

Education evolves

By the time Elizabeth Sides resigned from the position of education officer in 1993, the critical role of education was established in the Zoo. Primary school teacher, Michelle Griffin succeeded her and was assisted by Úna Smyth from 1994. Providing an educational experience for the busloads of primary school children who visited between April and June was still the big challenge. Úna Smyth recalled:

> Although most of the students and teachers would have received worksheets from us in advance, they were very much left to their own devices. At that time, there was no fence around the lake and we were lucky that no one fell in. It was very difficult to give teachers and young students a worthwhile experience and whatever the students learnt was down to the interest and enthusiasm of their own teachers.

Michelle and Úna introduced an annual accredited in-service training day for primary school teachers, which filled to capacity each year. It allowed them to spread knowledge to the teachers, who would then pass it on to their students with the help of the Dublin Zoo educational packages. Meanwhile they did their best to meet as many students as possible and deliver a short talk and slide show in Haughton House, but with tens of thousands of students coming in, it was only possible to connect with a small percentage of them.

In the mid-1990s, the team turned their attention to the secondary school students. This was a more challenging market because there would need to be a practical link to the curriculum to attract interest from teachers. The introduction of the national Transition Year programme to the mainstream curriculum in 1994–1995 created an opportunity, and Dublin

Elephants Judy (left) and Kirsty with keepers Ken Mackey (left) and Gerry Creighton (junior).

The last of the African lions in Dublin Zoo: Matt (1983–2008) and Sheila (1987–2012).

Zoo's Education Department was one of the first of the national institutions to provide an educational programme that linked directly to the new syllabus. The team focused its message on animal conservation and the challenges faced by the animals in the wild with particular reference to species kept in Dublin Zoo. By 2000 the resources available to the educators were still very limited but the direction in which the Education Department was going was in keeping with the best international standards.[24]

African Plains

In June 1997, Fianna Fáil was voted back into office and Bertie Ahern was now Taoiseach. His continued interest in the Zoo led to an extraordinary development. For decades Dublin Zoo's management had been asking for more land and getting nowhere but with the Doyle Report's recommendation that the Zoo's property be extended, Peter Wilson was able to lobby successfully for a substantial addition. In 1997, during the interregnum period following the resignation of President Mary Robinson on 12 September and before the inauguration of President Mary McAleese on

11 November, the government agreed to grant 13 hectares of land around the lake in Áras an Uachtaráin to the Zoo.[25] President Mary McAleese, on taking up office, approved the grant. This nearly doubled the size of the Zoo and was a huge achievement for Peter Wilson and the council.

Martin Heffernan once more headed up the design team to develop this area. The decision was made to call it the African Plains and transfer African animals to the new space. There was enough money to provide extensive open exhibits and good night facilities for the animals. There was also scope for a substantial mixed exhibit where giraffe, ostrich, zebra and oryx could share the same space. As each exhibit was completed, rhinoceros, hippopotamus, lions, chimps, bongos and other animals were released into large, spacious areas.

With buildings kept to a minimum, landscaping and foliage were critical elements in the design of the animals' habitats. Stephen Butler and the horticulture team were challenged to provide plants that could be included in or around the exhibits but would not be eaten, trampled on or knocked over by the animals. They also had to select plants that were either native to the African plains or had a visual resemblance to African species. One of these was the false acacia, a North American tree that looked like the African acacia but which would be viable in Ireland's climate.

The African Plains was opened in July 2000 by Taoiseach Bertie Ahern. By then the mixed exhibit with the giraffe and zebra was complete and the hippo exhibit was also complete. At the event, Bertie Ahern announced that a further £2 million a year for five years would be granted to the Zoo to continue its development. Dublin Zoo once more had a solid base from which it could grow and take its place amongst the best zoos in the world. In 2009, council member Dorothy Kilroy said, 'We owe Bertie Ahern a huge debt of gratitude'.

Visitor numbers from 1980–2000. The spikes in 1986 and 1993 were due to the visit of the giant pandas and the Dino Live exhibition respectively. The dip in 1995 was due to the major infrastructural works in the Zoo.

Chapter 7

Towards a Conservation Zoo
2000–2018

Summary

The transformation that Dublin Zoo went through during this period was extraordinary. With government support, additional land, a committed professional team and public support, the Zoo's management had much to work with. There were also great challenges, especially as the international zoo community was relying on individual zoos to explore and share ideas on how zoos could convey urgent messages about biodiversity, animal conservation and environmental awareness to their visitors.

In 2006, after consolidating its infrastructure, Dublin Zoo announced a visionary master plan. The new habitats attracted international attention, among them the Gorilla Rainforest which was cited by the World Association of Zoos and Aquariums as an example of how to design zoo habitats with the highest animal welfare standards in mind. The skills and expertise of the staff drew colleagues from around the world to study Dublin Zoo husbandry, management, habitat design and horticulture. Visitor numbers soared to over a million each year from 2011 onwards despite a deep recession. And with every aspect of its operations working towards the same goals, Dublin Zoo became a national centre for the promotion of animal conservation as well as being the most popular family day out in Ireland.

The new century

The extension of the Zoo, called the African Plains, was formally opened in July 2000 with an expansive habitat for giraffe, oryx, zebra and ostrich. It was the first mixed habitat in the Zoo and required thought and observation to ensure that the species worked well together. Society members and annual pass holders were

invited to a special viewing and, to the astonishment of staff who expected about 500 people to show up, over 8,500 people attended. Even the exceptional nine-week closure of the Zoo in spring 2001 due to the national foot-and-mouth disease emergency did not dampen optimism for the future.

In October, director Peter Wilson retired from position of director. During his 17-year directorship he had successfully steered the Zoo through its most serious financial crisis since the Great Famine in 1845–1850.

He had shifted responsibility for the operations of the Zoo away from the council to professional staff, and positioned the council as the overseeing authority. He had established the vision of the Zoo as a centre for conservation and education with the plan published in 1994 and had set up key departments, including education, animal registration and marketing. He had also overseen a redundancy and retirement programme, and introduced external training for keepers.

Aware of the complex demands that would be placed

Keeper Susan O'Brien with male bongo, Bura, in the African Plains.

on Peter Wilson's successor, the council organised a global search for a replacement. Leo Oosterweghel, who had worked in zoos in the Netherlands and Australia and was most recently director of Melbourne Zoo, was appointed. In the course of his career, Oosterweghel had worked with some of the most innovative zoo master planners and animal husbandry experts. He had travelled extensively, spending time observing many species in their natural habitats. His vision of how a zoo could be a powerful centre for conservation education complemented the intentions of the Dublin Zoo council. His first step was to consolidate every aspect of the infrastructure of the Zoo.

The Zoo Team

Following the Dixon Room Agreement between management and staff in 1995, multi-skilled teams now took responsibility for designated regions of the Zoo. With an investment in equipment in 2002, work practices were mechanised to stop unsafe manual handling. At the same time, the old-fashioned approach to having different uniforms depending on

role ceased and now all outdoor staff wore a good-quality 'zoo-green' uniform while the volunteers wore a distinctive red fleece or jumper. The following year, advertisements for several new keeping positions attracted hundreds of applicants. As more women joined the keeping staff, the tradition of precluding them from working with large animals ended.

In 1999 the Zoo had linked up with Sparsholt College in Hampshire, England, a centre for certified training recognised by the British and Irish Association of Zoos and Aquariums (BIAZA). New staff were encouraged to undertake these courses and existing staff members were given the opportunity to attend modules of selected programmes. In October 2005 the council set up a budget for staff development including attendances at conferences and other professional meetings. The intention was to spread training and networking opportunities throughout the staff and bring benefits into every aspect of the Zoo's operations.

Several key appointments were made during this phase. In 2002 Tony Kearney was appointed financial controller. An accountant by profession, he was to keep a tight grip on the Zoo's finances. In February

Helen Clarke Bennett, African Plains team leader, who worked in the Zoo as a teenager and became a full-time keeper in 1987.

2004, Paul O'Donoghue was appointed assistant to the director (animals and grounds). He brought with him many years of experience working with wild animals in national parks in Africa and Malaysia, as well as in British and Australian zoos. A new building with offices, kitchens, showers, locker space, and a large communal eating area was completed in 2005. Besides giving all staff decent accommodation for the first time in the Zoo's history, the new facilities provided easy access to the computerised record-keeping system and to international resources such as Zootrition, which provides up-to-date information on nutrition for the animals. Computer courses were provided for staff. As time went on staff facilities closer to the animal habitats were built, allowing staff to remain close to their sections during the day.

The impact of the changes was soon evident. In 2004, Dublin Zoo was represented at the EAZA annual conference in Sweden by Helen Clarke, African Plains team leader; Gerry Creighton, team leader for elephants and the west side; and Eddie O'Brien, team leader for the east side, along with the director and the assistant to the director (animals and grounds). In October 2005

several keepers spoke at the British Association of Science Festival hosted by Trinity College Dublin. In May 2006, keepers Ciaran McMahon and Alice Cooper attended the International Congress of Zoo Keepers in Australia. Two years later, Gerry Creighton's paper entitled 'Giant Footsteps' about the new elephant habitat, the Kaziranga Forest Trail, was voted by delegates to the British and Irish Association of Zoos and Aquariums (BIAZA) conference as the best paper of the conference. And at Bristol Regional Environment Enrichment Conference in 2008, delegates selected the paper about the enrichment programme for elephants presented by keepers James Creighton and Alice Cooper as the best paper.

Visitor facilities

The quality of visitor facilities was also urgently addressed. With over 600,000 visitors in 2000, existing facilities were under severe pressure. In December 2001 Haughton House restaurant was closed following a spot check by the Eastern Health Board. A temporary restaurant was set up in a marquee on the lawn until the Meerkat Restaurant was opened in January 2005. The new restaurant featured a meerkat habitat that resembled the animals' semi-desert environment. Other crucial visitor facilities rolled out at this time included additional toilets, picnic tables and rubbish bins that would not shed their contents in high winds.

By now the reserved areas, private toilets and the exclusive social functions once associated with membership of the Zoological Society of Ireland had gone. Instead membership had become about free entry to the Zoo, receipt of a regular high-quality magazine *Zoo Matters* and a discount on event tickets. By 2000 membership had risen to over 12,000 and has remained constant year after year.

The polar bears

Although the new management team had a vision for the animals and habitats in Dublin Zoo, several projects went ahead before the integrated master plan was completed. The first of these was to help the distressed polar bears, Spunky and Ootec, who were still a cause of concern to staff and visitors. In 1997 they had been moved to a new exhibit as part of the Fringes of the Arctic development but a year later Spunky, the female, was still swimming repetitively. In 2002 Sophie Sharpe, an animal behaviouralist from

Waldrapp ibis in the Ibis Cliff, which was opened by An Taoiseach Bertie Ahern, September 2002.

Oxford University, studied them and concluded that 'the repetitive behaviour of the female bear might well be caused by the constant presence of the male.'[1] Using professional contacts through the European zoo network, Dublin Zoo learnt that a state-of-the-art habitat for polar bears was under construction in Sóstó Zoo in Hungary. The large habitat would have a substantial pool and two separate but interconnecting spaces where the females could get away from the males. Arrangements were made to transfer Spunky and Ootec there. In April 2003 they arrived and settled

in well, making extensive use of the pool. Spunky died in 2008, when she was at least 28 years old.

Another project that predated the master plan was the transformation of the recently-vacated chimpanzee enclosure near Haughton House for critically endangered waldrapp ibis being transferred from Twycross Zoo in England. In 2001 the new director Leo Oosterweghel suggested drawing on a real waldrapp ibis habitat for design inspiration. Using a photo of a cliff in Bireçik, Turkey, where the birds still live, plans were adjusted, terraced ledges with drainage and inbuilt heating were

Director Leo Oosterweghel (left) with An Taoiseach Bertie Ahern at the opening of the Kaziranga Forest Trail, in June 2007.

constructed, a creator of artificial rock was employed to match the colours of Bireçik, and foliage was planted. Three non-reflective windows were put in to allow visitors to look up at the cliff. This was the first time the design of a Dublin Zoo habitat had been inspired directly by the natural environment of one of the animals. It was a success, and two years later the birds raised two chicks. Since then, despite some interruptions caused by processes to protect them against bird flu, the waldrapp ibis in Dublin Zoo have thrived.

Master plan for Dublin Zoo

In 2005 the World Association of Zoos and Aquariums (WAZA) published a strategic document 'Building a future for wildlife'. By then the global organisation had more than 280 institutional members, which together attracted over 700 million visitors each year. WAZA's strategy contained practical ways in which zoos could communicate information about wild animals and promote a strong conservation message. The new vision and master plan for Dublin Zoo, launched in 2006, incorporated WAZA's strategic thinking and the most innovative zoo habitat design. Earlier in the year Taoiseach Bertie Ahern had announced an additional grant of €20 million over five years for further redevelopment, giving Dublin Zoo the money required to realise a truly ambitious master plan.

A formidable team of experts was gathered to prepare a document called *A Vision for Dublin Zoo*. It was led by the Zoo team, including management representing every aspect of the Zoo's operations. As government money was being used, funds were administered through the Office of Public Works (OPW). This gave the Zoo access to the professional services and processes required for successful development. Jones and Jones, a Seattle-based landscaping and architectural firm, was also invited to participate. Jones and Jones specialised in zoo design and had pioneered the 'realism and landscape immersion' concept for animal habitats in zoos. Leo Oosterweghel was familiar with their work from the award-winning 'Trail of Elephants' in Melbourne Zoo, completed in 2003. In these habitats, the animals' space replicated their wild habitat in so far as possible, encouraging behaviours and social groupings natural to the species. And the visitors' area evoked a sense of the animals' natural world with vegetation, twisting pathways and special features.

Dublin Zoo's 2006 master plan recommended that the Zoo be divided into several zoogeographical zones including an Asian and an African rainforest. Launching the plan, Taoiseach Bertie Ahern said:

> I am lucky to have witnessed at first hand the tremendous work, the vision and commitment of Peter Wilson, Leo Oosterweghel and all their team over the years... The development plans have been animal centred. They have been conservation centred. And remarkably they have been visitor centred too. And I say remarkably, because at the best of times, it is

difficult to realise a vision in which you have so many strands dovetailing with each other with one ultimate goal in mind.[2]

The Kaziranga Forest Trail

The first major habitat under the new master plan was the Kaziranga Forest Trail for the Asian elephant, an ambitious project with layers of complexity. Jones and Jones produced a schematic design for an immersive habitat, which was further developed by senior architect Kevin Wolahan and other professional staff from the OPW. The new habitat adopted the principles of 'protected contact', a recently developed elephant management style in which elephants lived in their own space and contact with the keepers was only through a specially designed fence. It allowed the elephants to maintain a natural social group with minimal interaction with the keepers; it was also much safer for the keepers. In taking this approach, Dublin Zoo was going to be one of the first zoos to build a new elephant facility entirely with protected contact in mind. International elephant experts Alan Roocroft, who had pioneered protected contact, and Martin van Wees of Rotterdam Zoo were called upon to help with detailed aspects of the design.

The new habitat was inspired by the Kaziranga Forest, a biodiversity hotspot in Assam, India, undisturbed by human presence and with a great range of wildlife, including elephants, tigers and the world's largest remaining population of Indian rhinoceros. This established a link between the wild and Dublin Zoo that could be used to support elephant conservation and deliver conservation messages to visitors. The Kaziranga Forest Trail, as the new habitat was called, was designed to accommodate a breeding group of elephants. Judy and Kirsty, the elephants then resident in Dublin Zoo, were older females and unlikely to breed. They were transferred to Neunkirchen Zoo in Germany, and three related female Asian elephants were transferred from Rotterdam Zoo. By now Dublin Zoo had full accreditation under the Balai Directive, a European Union directive that allows animals in accredited zoos to be transferred without quarantine or excessive paperwork. The family group, sisters Bernhardine and Yasmin and Bernhardine's daughter, Anak, were part of the European Association of Zoos and Aquaria (EAZA) Asian elephant breeding programme. Bernhardine and Yasmin were both pregnant when they arrived in Dublin. Alan Roocroft provided ongoing training to the keepers, helping Dublin Zoo to become one of the foremost exponents of protected contact in the world.

Critical to a successful herd was the design that allowed the elephants to live together day and night. Important features were introduced, notably a night house with two-metre deep sand so the elephants could create depressions in the sand and sleep comfortably

Asian elephant Bernhardine and her calf, Asha, born 2007. Asha was the first calf born in Dublin Zoo.

Above: (l-r) Asha, Budi and Anak going into the five-metre pool in the Kaziranga Forest Trail. **Left:** Curator of Horticulture Stephen Butler standing in the Kaziranga Forest Trail amongst the giant lily, *Cardiocrinum giganteum*, in 2010. Seeds of the giant lily, native to the Himalayas, were sown in the Zoo nursery in 2001. They take up to two years to germinate and another seven years to flower.

beside each other if they wished. In 2006–2007 this was surprisingly revolutionary; zoos were reluctant to introduce sand as a substrate because they believed it was difficult to clean despite the comfort it gave to the animals. There was also concern that the elephants would injure each other if they were not separated or chained at night. To minimise the danger of this, the elephant house had features that supported the elephants' comfort including hanging feed nets, plenty of food supplies on timers to allow for overnight feeding, sprinklers, natural light and 24-hour access to an outdoor area. The 8,000 square metres of outdoor

habitat was fitted with two deep pools, artificial rock to rub against, sand substrate, mud banks, hidden food supplies, a high-powered hose which would be used to spray the elephants on hot days, and other features and obstacles to support their natural behaviours.

Elephant births

Bernhardine's calf was due in summer 2007 and the birth was to take place within protected contact. At the time this was considered to be a risky approach; the herd would need to manage the birth by themselves and if anything went wrong, the keepers would be unable to intervene. As the expected arrival date drew closer, CCTV and infrared lights were installed in the elephant house and Leo Oosterweghel, Paul O'Donoghue, team leader Gerry Creighton and the elephant team followed the movements of the expecting mother Bernhardine on their laptops. Gerry Creighton described the night of the birth:

> We had a hint something was happening. [Bernhardine] was lifting her tail up, walking backwards and doing everything [the elephant expert] Alan Roocroft had told us she would do. I couldn't really sleep, I kept

looking at my laptop, which was relaying the CCTV from the elephant house. At midnight I realised something was happening and rang Alan, who was having dinner with friends in San Diego but was watching on his laptop too. I picked up [keeper] Alice [Cooper] on the way in. [Keeper] Ciaran [McMahon] was already at the Zoo. We were all in Leo's office at two in the morning – Leo, Paul [O'Donoghue]. There was tension in the room: is everything all right? Every time her tail twitched we reacted. We kept going with coffee. Alan was on the other end of the phone: 'Here she goes, baby entering the birth canal'. There was a large swelling under the tail but it still could be 24 hours before the baby arrived. Anak, the four-year-old, was following her around, sniffing Bernhardine. Then the baby came out. There was no movement for what felt like an eternity. Mam was doing everything great, ears flapping in excitement. But there was no movement. We had to make a decision: do we go up?

They remained in the director's office and eight minutes later the calf moved. It was a healthy female. The entire birth had taken place in total darkness with Yasmin and Anak nearby. The newborn took her first steps ten minutes after her birth. She was named Asha, meaning 'Hope' in Hindi following a public competition. The birth generated massive publicity

and visitor numbers soared from 750,000 in 2006 to 906,000 in 2007.

In 2008 Yasmin gave birth to a healthy male named Budi. Once more the birth was during the night and captured on CCTV with the elephant and management teams watching from nearby. Anak, now nearly five years old, worked with Bernhardine to help Yasmin with the birth while the calf Asha looked on. In 2008 Meike Artelt from the University of Vienna spent two weeks recording the vocal communication within the herd and concluded:

> They are the quietest herd I have studied so far. This is a good sign because it means they are a closely bonded, small, happy and relaxed family unit who communicate more in non-verbal ways. They seem to experience little or no stress and so panic and scared sounds are not in their repertoire.[3]

The African Savanna

The next major habitat to be undertaken was the African Savanna for the giraffe, zebra, ostrich and scimitar horned oryx. It was to be created by the transformation of the mixed habitat in the African Plains, which had been opened in 2000. Using government funding, the design team again included Jones and Jones as well as the OPW architects and the Zoo team. Creating a dry savanna landscape in Dublin was a challenge, but the Curator of Horticulture, Stephen Butler, chose

View of the African Savanna.

President Mary McAleese meeting guests at the opening of the African Savanna, April 2009.

grasses, plants, trees and shrubs to evoke a sense of the African savanna. The original intention was to mix the breeding group of southern white rhinoceros with the other animals in the African Savanna but the zebra and the rhinos were not compatible.

The rhinoceros herd consisted of three older animals that had been in the Zoo for some time and three animals that had been brought in from Africa in 2004 with the encouragement of the European studbook keeper. The younger animals, one male and two females, had been listed as surplus in South African parks and Paul O'Donoghue had gone there to select three unrelated animals of breeding age. Two of these mated and in May 2008 a lively female calf was born. The rhinoceros continued to breed well, introducing important new genes to the southern white rhinoceros population in European zoos.

Haughton House, events

While work on the big animal habitats was underway, smaller projects were being completed with help from the OPW. These included a new temporary Discovery and Learning Centre at Society House in 2006, refurbishment of the Nakuru restaurant in the African Plains in 2007, and secure 'Zoo green' fencing around the entire Zoo in 2008. In 2008 the Phoenix Park authorities of the OPW created an extensive car parking area to the west of the Zoo. With all of these projects, care was taken to incorporate the philosophy of conservation into every aspect of design and construction: materials used were environmentally friendly, animal representations in new playgrounds were respectful and accurate, signage was a thoughtful mix of information, and the skulls, horns, eggs and other biofacts and replicas added valuable educational experiences with the assistance of dedicated volunteers.

The most important of these ancillary projects was the transformation of Haughton House. Over the decades, extensions had swamped the building and the whole structure was in poor condition. In 2008 a splendid refurbishment of the building using government funding got underway. The building was returned close to its original footprint. Upstairs became an elegant meeting and function space where visitors could look out over the Zoo, and downstairs was turned into a small Discovery and Learning Centre devoted to the Asian elephant.

With Haughton House completed, Dublin Zoo was once more ready to host events but unlike the days of

Southern white rhino Nyala and her male calf Tadala.

Clockwise from top: Shane Brennan (left) and John Higgins of Moondance Productions filming in the Waldrapp Ibis Cliff for *The Zoo* television programme; Tony Kearney, financial controller from 2002 to 2015; Grace Hefferon at her wedding to Captain Kenneth Deegan in Dublin Zoo, August 2018.

exclusive privileges of members, now anyone could apply for public event tickets or to hire the facilities. A new position of events manager was created to reinvigorate this side of the Zoo's activities. The appointee, Aoife Keegan, began with birthday parties and moved on to corporate days, family gatherings and weddings. She worked with the volunteers and other members of the Zoo team to organise themed events such as the Valentine's Day breakfasts, St Patrick's Day events, Easter and Halloween events, and the ever-popular Santa's Grotto. The reintroduction of events was timely because many adults who attended events had not visited since childhood and were returning to see a transformed zoo.

Marketing the Zoo

In May 2009, Moondance Productions, a television production company, began filming a series of behind-the-scenes programmes about life in the Zoo. Over the years numerous broadcasting companies had expressed interest in making a series about the Zoo and only now was the Zoo ready to welcome in the cameras. Pembroke Communications, a public relations company, was appointed to support the

Horticulture team, (l-r), Pat Kane, Mark Mooney, Joxan Garcia, Jimmy Prior, Chris Fusco and curator Stephen Butler.

Zoo's three-person Marketing Department. Shane Brennan and John Higgins of Moondance gained the trust and cooperation of the staff and the first series of six 25-minute episodes was broadcast on TV3 in spring 2010. The second and subsequent series were each ten episodes long and were broadcast on RTÉ One with repeats during the year. Although *The Zoo* was made primarily for an Irish market, it was also broadcast on the Discovery Channel and in several countries including Belgium where it was especially popular. It was also used for in-flight entertainment by Aer Lingus. By 2018 there had been seven series with another in preparation.

The Zoo was an enormous departure for Dublin Zoo in many respects. For the first time the keepers rather than senior management spoke directly to the camera. They were filmed going about their daily routines as they talked knowledgably about what they were doing. This was the beginning of a carefully devised marketing strategy that maintained the Zoo's role as a great family day out while presenting increasingly sophisticated messages about animal conservation and environmental awareness. The intention was to educate and inform, to give an insight into the level of consideration that went into animal welfare and husbandry in Dublin Zoo, to explain how the animals are cared for and to show the enthusiasm and passion of the keepers. The big stories were covered; births,

introductions, animal transfers to other zoos, medical procedures and deaths. Over time viewers were taken into the complexity of the studbook system and how animals, even well-loved ones like Budi the elephant calf born in the Zoo in 2008, were not owned by one institution but were part of a European or even global population and may have to leave Dublin for another zoo. And with each series, there was plenty of additional media coverage.

Gerry Creighton, Operations Manager, said:

> The transparency in the TV show is incredible. A lot of zoos wouldn't let that happen. You see the trials and tribulations of zoo life, you see animals dying. You see a macaque when she gave birth carrying her dead baby around, which she does because of the very strong bond between mother and young. But the explanation as to what is happening and why the animal is behaving like that is presented there in black and white so that viewers can understand too.

The recession

By the time *The Zoo* was first broadcast, Ireland had sunk into a deep economic recession that became progressively more severe. Previous economic

White-naped mangabey and young.

recessions had brought the Zoo, a self-funding charity, to the brink of disaster but this time was different. *The Zoo* television programme was generating new interest in Dublin Zoo and was turning animals and keepers into stars. The Marketing Department, under the skilful management of Emma Kiernan since January 2011, provided beautiful photographs and footage of recent animal births to the media. Social media kept the growing number of followers up to date, and strategic promotions with media outlets used different ways to add value to the price of a family ticket. In 2010 more than 960,000 people came to the Zoo and the following year the Zoo reached the magical number of 1,000,000 visitors. It was the top visitor attraction in the Republic of Ireland in 2011. Shaun Quinn of Fáilte Ireland explained, 'As more Irish people stayed at home in 2010, it is no surprise that family friendly attractions such as the Zoo and Fota Wildlife Park actually recorded significant increases'.[4]

But there were other reasons why Dublin Zoo survived the recession so well. One of these was the way in which the Zoo's finances had been handled during the boom when, for the first time in the Zoo's history, there were generous grants from the government and excellent income from gate receipts. Despite the comparative wealth, the council maintained the same degree of frugality it had done for the previous 180 years, discussing every proposal, monitoring the spending of the government funds and making sure there was no wastage. Tony Kearney, financial controller from 2002–2015, put processes in place to maximise savings in purchasing, streamline human resource policies and tidy up outstanding legal matters. Administrative staff levels were kept to a minimum and outsourced activities scrutinised carefully.

As the recession deepened and the outstanding capital funding was reduced by 25 per cent, the systems, processes and efficiencies were so well established that financially the Zoo remained strong. The remaining capital funding was assigned to building a spacious storehouse, a horticultural facility with a green house, veterinary and quarantine facilities, and a waste management area. It was also used to construct the elephant bull house to complete the Kaziranga Forest Trail project. The OPW was involved in all of these projects, which were completed to a very high standard.

Meanwhile good entrance receipts were creating a surplus that could be used for new habitats. In addition, the Zoo as a brand was attracting the attention of prestigious companies that were interested

John Bainbridge, veterinary surgeon, Dublin Zoo, 1994–2018

John Bainbridge worked as the consulting veterinary surgeon to Dublin Zoo from 1994 to 2018.

When I arrived, the veterinary clinic was one room in the old yard and had practically no equipment. I was in companion animal practice in Dublin and had no experience with exotic animals. The previous vet had already left the country so there was no one to refer to. I used my time off to visit zoos in Britain and Europe. For the following ten or fifteen years, I spent my holidays in zoos with good veterinary departments. These included San Diego Zoo, Taronga in Sydney, Melbourne Zoo and Singapore Zoo. My family would head off to the beach and I would work with the vets. I also attended international conferences and congresses, and kept up to date with the professional literature. I found out what other zoos were doing, learnt about their specialisations and interests and developed a network, which I could draw on when necessary. The international veterinary community was – and still is – very supportive and more than happy to help.

As a vet, I am a general practitioner. I carried out a lot of procedures at Dublin Zoo. However when it came to specialised support, I would find and coordinate the experts, who sometimes came in from Britain or Europe. I could also draw on the UCD Veterinary Hospital team who did all the x-ray work, blood tests, complicated anaesthetics and surgery. UCD also carried out all the post-mortem examinations and pathology work.

Over the years, the Dublin Zoo team has developed expertise in the species that it holds. I became familiar early on with the chimps as we would have used basic anaesthetics to move them from the bear pit in the old part of the Zoo to the islands in the African Plains in 2000. During the 25 years that I have been with the Zoo, the drugs have become much better. The expertise of the Animal Care team has also advanced and veterinary work is very much team work. We have improved our handling of the animals and we have developed expertise in some of those complicated procedures including giraffe anaesthetics. In 2011 I was involved in designing the new high-quality veterinary surgery and excellent quarantine facilities in Dublin Zoo, which was built with the aid of a government grant.

Throughout this time I continued on with my practice and would go to Dublin Zoo routinely three days a week or when there was an emergency. I am in contact with the new veterinary consultant to pass on my experience and to share links into the international network.

in sponsoring an aspect of its work or entering into partnerships. These included Agri Aware with Family Farm, Fyffes with the new Gorilla Rainforest, and the Natural Confectionery Company with The Kaziranga Forest Trail, as well as McVitie's Penguin bar supporting the Penguin habitat and Kellogg's Coco Pops contributing towards the South America house.

Family Farm

In 2010, the Zoo established a partnership with the Agricultural Awareness Trust, or Agri Aware, to create 'Family Farm', an up-to-date manifestation of Pets' Corner. Redesigned by Jones and Jones with the Zoo team, an acre of land was cleverly transformed into Ireland's smallest farm with corrals for pigs, sheep and cows, goats, geese and hens, and a substantial

farmhouse school, all surrounded by a meadow and hedgerow. Everything was on a scale to make a four-year-old feel welcome. A milking cow and a beef cow, lent by farmers, were often on hand to show the differences in size between the two. The Horticulture team planted a herbaceous border of native plants around Family Farm to encourage insects, birds and summer flowers.

Agri Aware's interest in supporting this venture was to promote a greater understanding of farming in Ireland. For several years, they successfully bid for European funds to deliver a communication campaign about the Common Agriculture Policy (CAP) in the Zoo. During the summer, they sponsored young farmers who demonstrated farming skills, and crafts people who showed traditional skills including basket weaving, sheep shearing and butter churning. Family Farm

Clockwise from top left: Piglets in Family Farm; Cliona Magerusan (age 2) in Family Farm vegetable garden; Actor, Tony Tormey, who sat on an elephant in Dublin Zoo with singer Sean Dunphy in 1967 to promote the Irish Eurovision entry *If I could choose*. With his family (l-r) Kate, Issy and Max at the 'Poetry Wall' in Family Farm in 2019. From 2014, unused walls of buildings were chosen to bring nature-themed poetry to the Zoo; Marian Reece with her daughter Bróna (Fletcher) and granddaughter Lydia-Rose on the wishing chair in 2015 in Family Farm.

Harry, silverback gorilla, 1986–2016. He arrived in Dublin Zoo in 1995.

remains busy all year round with events for parents and toddlers scheduled for the quieter months, and classes delivered by an Agri Aware teacher to schoolchildren.

Gorilla Rainforest

The next ambitious animal habitat was the Gorilla Rainforest, which was opened in September 2011 by President Mary McAleese. The western lowland gorillas in Dublin Zoo had been living in the 1971 ape house since 1986. Modifications had improved their conditions and given them some privacy but a new habitat had been a priority for some time. Jones and Jones again worked with the Zoo team on the design of the new 7,000 square metre habitat embedded in another 5,000 square metres of natural landscape in the African Plains. Donal Higgins and his engineering consulting firm Hayes Higgins Partnership, who had worked on previous projects in the Zoo, took over from the OPW as project managers for Dublin Zoo's large developments. The animals' natural environment in the Democratic Republic of the Congo was the inspiration and soon the Dublin Zoo gorillas

were moved into a landscape with high outcrops, slopes, trees and dense vegetation. Swampy areas formed several islands, some of which only have a fallen tree trunk as a crossing. A water course separated the winding visitor path from the gorilla habitat.

The Irish based company, Fyffes, fruit importer and distributor, contributed a substantial amount of money towards the gorilla rainforest and promoted Dublin Zoo on the packaging of its bananas, which were for sale throughout the country. Marketing manager Emma Kiernan said, 'It was a really lovely sponsorship. They matched our values as a family-friendly company that wanted to promote healthy eating to all ages.'

The gorillas settled into their new habitat very well. In April 2016 two four-year-old gorillas, a male and a female, were received from Wilhelma Zoo in Stuttgart, which specialises in hand-raising great apes. The decision to transfer these animals to Dublin was based on the size and quality of the Gorilla Rainforest, and the tolerant and accepting nature of the Zoo's silverback, Harry. But shortly after they arrived, Harry died suddenly of a stroke at the age of 30. The outpouring of

The Gorilla Rainforest and horticulture

For Curator of Horticulture Stephen Butler and his team, this was their largest project to date. After much research, they planted 15,000 shrubs, trees, water plants, marshy plants and herbaceous plants, as well as grass and wildflower seeds. For the part of the habitat where the gorillas lived it was necessary to select species that they would not eat or damage easily. One of the plants selected was a willow species, the *Salix purpurea*. Dublin's gorillas had different species of willow in their browse but Butler was aware that the *Salix purpurea* was avoided by wild rabbits so he decided to try it in the Gorilla Rainforest:

> When the gorillas moved into the habitat, I watched one of them pull this willow out of the ground, strip it, and put it into its mouth. Then to my relief the animal spat it out. The gorillas quickly learnt that it did not taste nice. They played with it, broke it down but then left it alone. We knew that they might eat it if they had nothing else so the Animal Care team makes sure they have plenty of other food.

But one spring, Butler noticed something unexpected:

> The red-capped mangabeys were sharing the habitat with the gorillas. It was April and I watched a mangabey bend one of the willows down, strip it and eat it. It was flowering with two-inch catkins. I got out the binoculars. I could see the mangabey was eating the flower but not the leaves. The flower is sweet and full of nectar. I went around to the other side of the hill and saw that the gorillas were doing the same thing. Their chins were green as they stuffed the catkins into their mouths. I don't know who taught who what; did the mangabeys work it out and the gorillas copy them? As soon as the willow stopped flowering, they all left it alone. Although taking the catkins does a little damage to the plant, they won't get every flower so it is not a long-term problem.

Butler entered his observations on Zooplants.net, a database created by zoo horticulturalists to share information about useful plants for animal habitats in zoos.

Mayani in the Gorilla Rainforest
shortly after it was opened in 2011.

Gorillas, Lena and Kituba in the
Gorilla Rainforest, which was
opened in 2011.

sympathy, grief and support for Harry and the Dublin
Zoo team was unprecedented. The press coverage was
huge and the Dublin Zoo Facebook post was viewed by
over 1.4 million people within 24 hours.

The Animal Care team had to manage the situation.
Lena had been Harry's mate for 21 years and was close
to giving birth. She became more assertive and the
troop settled down, displaying harmonious behaviour.
Two years later in summer 2018, 36-year-old Lena died
after a short illness. Just before her death, Bangui, a
nine-year-old gorilla arrived from France to become
the future leader of a troop that is anticipated to grow
to 10-12 gorillas over the coming years. He settled in
well and within weeks had mated with three of the
females. His first born arrived in April 2019.

The Gorilla Rainforest received worldwide
recognition. In 2015, the World Association of Zoos
and Aquariums (WAZA) produced its animal welfare
strategy, 'Caring for Wildlife' to provide guidance to the

world's zoos on how to establish and maintain acceptable
animal welfare standards. The Gorilla Rainforest was one
of the two case studies used to describe innovative habitat
design, stating that it is 'unique in the way it matches
respect of existing landscape and the behavioural history
of western lowland gorillas, and successfully recreates
the character of their home place'.

Lions

In 2012, Sheila, the last of Dublin Zoo's non-provenanced
African lions, died. She was born in Dublin in 1987.
Matt, her companion for many years, had died in 2008.
Dublin Zoo had already declared its interest in breeding
the endangered Asian lion, of which there are only
about 500 left in the wild. The studbook keeper had
identified two Asian lion females for a possible move to
Dublin but under rigid studbook rules, the Zoo could
not have Asian and African lions at the same time even

African Plains team 2019 (l-r): Gretchen Doyle, Pamela O'Brien, Helen Clarke, John McGuinness, Ciara Tiernan, Ken Mackey, Thomas Munslow, J.P. Cranny, Jenny Darley.

if they were to be kept some distance apart. This was to ensure the purity of the bloodlines and to prevent the spread of disease. Although at 22 years, Sheila was considered old by standards in the wild, she was content and in good health. In 2012, Sheila went into decline and in August, the decision was made to euthanise her for reasons of animal welfare. Most of the Animal Care team was present during the procedure. Many of them had known her for their entire working life and there was considerable sadness at her passing. Moondance featured the whole process in *The Zoo* television programme, from the discussion about the quality of her life, the decision to euthanise, to her final moments.

Earlier in the year, work on the new Asian Forests habitat near the Zoo entrance had been undertaken. Once more designed by Jones and Jones with the Dublin Zoo team, the habitat was inspired by the Gir Forest in India where the last remaining population of Asian lions live. It was ready to receive animals in March 2012 and, aware that Sheila was ailing, the studbook keeper allowed the two female Asian lions to come to Dublin Zoo under strict quarantine conditions. Sisters Suri and Sita settled in well and were joined by Kumar, a magnificent male from Rotterdam Zoo, in 2013. In 2017 Kumar was transferred to Frankfurt Zoo after fathering four healthy young cubs. Many visitors wished him a safe journey and posted their images of him on social media.

End of direct contact with the animals

In 2013 another long-standing tradition came to an end. In August a visitor and her young daughter were given keeper-supervised access to the tapirs. The tapirs were docile and there was no anticipation of danger. On this occasion, however, Rio, the female, bit the child and then bit the mother when she tried to protect her daughter. They were treated for their injuries in hospital and made a full recovery. There were formal investigations arising out of which Dublin Zoo was prosecuted by the Health and Safety Authority and fined without conviction. While it was acknowledged that close encounters with the Zoo's animals had been popular with visitors for a very long time, it was decided that all direct contact between visitors and animals should cease.

Asian elephants

In 2012, five years after it opened, the Kaziranga Forest Trail was proving to be very successful. The five elephants were well integrated as a herd, the mothers looking after the two calves and Anak growing up, sometimes playing with the calves, sometimes strolling with the adults. Zoo professionals were coming from all over the world to see protected contact with elephants in operation. Consultant Alan Roocroft provided training to the team several times a year, developing their skills, working

Asian lioness, Suri,
with male cub, 2014.

Brazilian tapir, Rio, with male calf, 2013.

with them to care for the mothers and calves, and devising ways to enrich the lives of the entire herd. Gerry Creighton, by now Operations Manager, was invited to address international audiences on the implementation and development of this pioneering approach to elephant management. Now the Zoo was ready to take it to the next step by introducing a bull elephant in the hope that he would mate with the adult females.

Before the bull arrived, the team had to make the decision to transfer Budi, born in Dublin Zoo in 2008, out of the Zoo to a young bachelor herd. The team were concerned about how an unrelated adult bull would respond to him. With extensive training, his transfer to Antwerp was carried out without stress to the animal, although several of the team who knew him so well were upset to see him go. In 2013 he went to live in a bachelor herd in Denver Zoo, United States, where his bloodline will bring fresh genes to the American zoo herds.

A state-of-the-art bull house with natural light and a deep sand floor was built with the last of the government funding. Alan Roocroft advised on the design for safety, access and the elephants' comfort.

Upali, a three-metre-tall, five-ton, 17-year-old bull from Chester Zoo, was selected to come to Dublin, arriving July 2012. He had sired several calves and was known to be a social animal that was tolerant with young elephants. Preparation for his arrival was intense and several members of the Dublin Zoo team spent time in Chester getting to know him. The introduction to the females was to be carried out in protected contact so there would be no way of intervening if there was trouble. Upali arrived at midnight on 6 July following a journey on boat and truck in a specially designed container. Three days later he was introduced to the females. The team watched closely as Upali calmly approached the females who responded to him with loud trumpeting, ear flapping, urinating, raised tails, smelling each other, touching and making other gestures that suggested excitement. Asha, who had never been in the presence of a bull before, followed the lead of the other three and showed no fear.

Over the following weeks, the females followed Upali around the habitat. The team took a calculated risk and allowed the females access to the bull house overnight.

Above: Asian bull elephant, Upali, greeting Yasmin and her daughter Anak for the first time, July 2012. **Below:** Mothers and calves, 2015. (l-r) Bernhardine, Avani, Asha, Kabir, Yasmin and Anak.

If there was any conflict between the elephants, some could get hurt and there would be no keepers around to distract them. Preparation was thorough: the two exits from the house were left open so the females could not be trapped by the bull and plenty of food was supplied so there would be no competition. The subsequent CCTV images showed them all sleeping close together. This was considered an important breakthrough in zoo management of elephants. Soon Upali had mated with Yasmin, Bernhardine and Anak and, with a 22-month gestation period, a baby boom could be expected in 2014, all going well.

Year of the elephants

Social media kept the public up to date with the pregnancies, which was another risky strategy because if anything went wrong, the Zoo had to be ready to handle negative publicity. But everything went very well. In July Yasmin gave birth to a male calf during the night. The other three females stayed close and showed great interest in the birth. The movement of the herd was captured on CCTV and their trumpeting, loud calls and grunts were recorded by radio producer, Colette Kinsella. In August Anak gave birth to a male calf. And in September Bernhardine gave birth to a female calf. The excitement

(L-r): Kavi, Ashoka and Samiya, all one year old in 2015.

that accompanied each of the problem-free births could be heard throughout the Zoo but the team stayed away, watching on CCTV at home as each calf arrived.

The Zoo's small marketing department launched the biggest campaign in the Zoo's history. It started during the later stages of the pregnancies and culminated in a month-long celebration of the elephants across the city in October. Dublin City Council joined with sponsors The Natural Confectionery Company and with Dublin Zoo to promote the 'Month of the Elephant' campaign. Flags, banners and posters were placed around the city, elephant images appeared in iconic locations and there was a weekend celebration across Dublin. Print and broadcast media joined in. The *Irish Independent* published a 32-page supplement about

Dublin's elephants which was given to every primary school student in the city, and a family day pass was given to everyone in the audience at the Late Late Show on RTÉ television. The following year, against very stiff opposition, Dublin Zoo won the prestigious All Ireland Marketing Award 2015 for the best public relations campaign for this promotion. Visitor figures in 2014 reached a new record of 1,076,876.

The successful breeding of elephants continued. By 2018 there were 11 elephants in the herd. The four young bulls were growing up and, like Budi before them, would soon become challenging for the herd to manage. In addition, Upali could not be allowed to breed in Dublin again and in February 2019 he was successfully moved to Le Pal Animal Park in France.

Top: Asian elephant Anak and her calf Sanjay. **Above**: The elephant team 2019 (l-r): Raymond Menzel, Christina Murphy, Anne Pennie, Gerry Creighton, Rosa Capatino, Anthony McClure, Karen Careighy and Gerard Corbally.

Rothschild giraffes Seanin, born 2007, and his half-brother, Tafari, born 2014.

International controversy

The Zoo's confidence in its visitors' understanding of its work was put to the test in 2014 when Copenhagen Zoo killed a healthy two-year-old giraffe named Marius because he did not fit into the global conservation plan for the species. There was an international outcry at the killing, especially as Copenhagen had announced its intentions in advance and ignored the petitions and protests to save him; it even rejected offers from several zoos to take Marius. To exacerbate matters, following his death, the giraffe was dissected in front of schoolchildren and fed to the Copenhagen zoo's lions. This was the first time widespread publicity had been given to the use of culling in some zoos to manage a conservation population. Conservation as an objective was first identified in the 1960s but the killing of Marius opened up the discussion about how animal conservation in zoos was working out in reality. Traditionally zoos did not criticise each other and the European Association of Zoos and Aquaria (EAZA) came out in support of Copenhagen Zoo. But some zoos publicly expressed their concern or even abhorrence at the killing of the healthy young animal. A gulf opened up between those that regarded zoo animals as specimens in a scientific breeding programme and those who regarded each animal as a sentient being to be cared for.

While the international controversy raged, a senior member of EAZA based in Amsterdam did an interview with RTÉ Radio 1 and spoke in support of Copenhagen's killing of Marius, explaining that his death was necessary for the long-term conservation of the species. Dublin Zoo had to respond immediately. Accepting that the Zoo's views might jeopardise professional relationships in the British and European zoo community, director Leo Oosterweghel did not mince his words. He condemned the killing in an unprecedented opinion piece in the *Irish Independent*. In it he said:

> Cold, calculated, cynical and callous. These are the words I would use to describe the events that occurred earlier this week in Copenhagen Zoo. The Marius case pushes the debate around animal welfare to the fore and the lens is now firmly focused on zoo ethics... Other zoos in the UK, continental Europe and

the Middle East offered to house the giraffe and it could have lived out its life... If a zoo has a mission to cultivate respect for wildlife then respect for the individual is inherent to that.

When commercialisation takes over in a zoo, ethics can become clouded. The same applies to science. Too much science can cloud ethics. It is my strong view that animal welfare should always outweigh commercial and scientific interest, as it does in Dublin Zoo. A zoo should lead by example and show kindness and empathy to wildlife.

In his annual report for 2014, the director further noted that a great amount of damage has been done to the social licence under which zoos operate, adding that Dublin Zoo was fully committed to contributing to a more intelligent and compassionate way of dealing with animals in the care of the global zoo community. Dublin Zoo was quoted in the Wikipedia entry about Marius as one of the zoos that condemned the killing of the young giraffe.

The controversy about culling healthy animals for conservation programmes continued, and is set to continue as the role of zoos in animal conservation matures. With greater success in breeding animals in zoos, with natural habitats still being eroded and with few practical programmes for reintroducing species to the wild, so the international zoo community is still grappling with how to deal with their breeding success. Several countries including Germany have legislation to outlaw the killing of healthy animals in zoos; in Ireland culling in zoos is legally allowed as a last resort. However Dublin Zoo has maintained its own stance on the subject, repeatedly stating that healthy animals are not to be culled.

Developing visitor awareness

Following the death of Marius and the ensuing controversy, Dublin Zoo received many distressed and angry queries and emails from visitors of all ages, including children. The director noted in his report to the council,

The reverberations from the Copenhagen action are echoing a generally uneasy public perception of zoos that lies just below the

Sulawesi crested macaques, 2011, with Sumo, the dominant male, on the right.

The Marketing team (l-r): Georgia Cooney, Aoibheann O'Flynn, Emma Kiernan, Suzanne O'Donovan and Angela Conroy.

Keeper Ken Mackey assisting in field work during a trip to the Lowveld Rhino Trust in Zimbabwe, 2014.

The challenges of placing males in conservation programmes

Team leader Ciaran McMahon and the West Side team were confronted with a dilemma when they were notified by the studbook keeper that Sumo, the alpha male Sulawesi crested macaque, was genetically over-represented in the conservation population and he should be removed from the Dublin troop. Sumo had arrived in Dublin in 2009 and, in May 2010 fathered the first of six healthy young. The troop lived on an island near the Zoo entrance. To prevent him from breeding any further, Sumo was transferred to the animal holding facility (formerly the gorilla house) along with two non-breeding females for company.

With the help of the studbook keeper, Dublin Zoo registrar/research and conservation coordinator, Sandra Molloy, launched a thorough search to find a suitable new home for Sumo. Molloy listed him as an available non-breeding animal and monitored that list regularly. Then in March 2017, Drayton Manor in Britain put out a call for some elderly macaques. They hoped to participate in the international breeding programme of the Sulawesi crested macaque in the future but wanted to learn more about them by caring for a non-breeding group. It was a perfect situation for Sumo, and he and his two female companions were transferred there where they can live out their lives.

surface. Often after such an event there will be increasingly steely-eyed examination of the way zoos operate... Dublin Zoo must insist on a sharpening up of ethics and help the zoo community steer towards a more intelligent and compassionate way in dealing with animals.

Dublin Zoo had long been aware of the fragility of the social licence under which zoos operate. Through transparency in its operations, strategic marketing and educational programmes, it encouraged visitor interest and knowledge. *The Zoo* television series and marketing strategy had undoubtedly been important in achieving this level of awareness. Marketing manager Emma Kiernan who oversaw the development of the programme said:

> The TV series has been based on solid building blocks to bring people along on the conservation journey. We started off to give an insight into how we care for animals here, the passion the keepers have, and the level of consideration that goes into animal welfare and husbandry in Dublin Zoo. Then we went to the next stage and talked about studbook keeping, how animals are transferred and how we don't buy or sell animals any more. And from there we brought the viewers to *in situ* conservation projects that Dublin Zoo supported and showed the problems the

animals are facing in the wild and the work that is going on there and how our visitors can help.

Bringing viewers to *in situ* conservation projects began with Series 4 of *The Zoo*, broadcast in 2013. A feature of the programme was footage taken by keeper Brendan Walsh of orangutans in Kalimantan, Indonesia. With support from Dublin Zoo, he travelled to Camp Leakey in the Tanjung Puting National Park and shared his joy at seeing the magnificent apes in the wild. The following series featured Susan O'Brien visiting the Golden Lion Tamarin Association in the Atlantic rainforests of Brazil, this time with a crew from Moondance. Susan's hosts told her that they had re-introduced 150 zoo-bred golden lion tamarins and there were now 1,700 of them in the wild. This had been achieved with the help of zoos including Dublin Zoo, which had been financially supporting the Association since 2000. Then they brought her to a vast expanse of burnt-out habitat caused by a deliberately-lit fire that had gone out of control. Through her eyes, Irish viewers were seeing the destruction that was eroding animal habitats in the wild.

Later that year keeper Ken Mackey and Moondance visited the Lowveld Rhino Trust in Zimbabwe, another *in situ* project supported by Dublin Zoo. Ken was well known to viewers for his work with the rhinoceros in the African Savanna but had never seen them in the wild. During his visit he worked with the *in situ* staff as they sedated a rhino, sawed off its horn, then monitored it as it came around and ran off into the bush. This, he was told on camera, was one of the ways in which the rangers were trying to discourage poachers. At the time rhino horn was worth more than gold in weight in Asia where, it was believed, it could cure many illnesses. Ken was well aware of the problem because rhinos in European zoos had been threatened. Dublin Zoo had even refused the offer of rhino horns seized by customs officials at Dublin Airport for fear that the Discovery and Learning Centre would become a target for thieves. The caution was warranted; in 2017 criminals shot a rhinoceros in a French zoo and removed its horn; a gang of Irish criminals was suspected of being involved.

Staff accompanied by Moondance went to several more *in situ* projects financially supported by Dublin Zoo over the following years. In 2015 team leader Helen Clarke Bennett went to Mbeli Bai, a conservation programme in the Democratic Republic of the Congo, to see western lowland gorillas. In 2017, team leader Ciaran McMahon and keeper Aisleen Greene travelled to Kalimantan in Indonesia to see the problems faced by the Orangutan Foundation in Pangkalan Bun. The same year registrar/research

and conservation coordinator Sandra Molloy visited Selamatkan Yaki in Sulawesi to see Sulawesi crested macaques in the wild. And in 2018 Gerry Creighton went to the Kaziranga National Park in Assam, India, with Moondance capturing footage of the biodiversity of animals and plants, and visited local communities to understand more about the conflict between human and elephant.

Sea Lion Cove and Flamingo Lagoon

Meanwhile the implementation of the 2006 master plan continued with ambitious habitats opening in time for the summer in 2015, 2016 and 2017. The first of these was the Pacific Coast with the Sea Lion Cove for the California sea lions and the Flamingo Lagoon for Chilean flamingos. The Sea Lion Cove was inspired by the natural environment of the California sea lions and designed by Jones and Jones with the Zoo team. It incorporated an area of the old sea lion pool and a portion of the lake. Sand-coloured stone and hundreds of plants, trees and shrubs in the surrounding landscape lend a sense of the Californian coastline. Now using only salt water with 63 inlets to create movement, the pool has islands, small caves and several different

Californian sea lion swimming in the salt water of the Sea Lion Cove, opened June 2015.

Californian sea lions looking at young visitor in the Sea Lion Cove.

President Michael D. Higgins and Sabina Higgins with the East Side team at opening of the Sea Lion Cove in June 2015. Front row (l-r): team leader Eddie O'Brien, Susan O'Brien, Pamela O'Brien, President Higgins, Mrs Higgins, Aisling Kenneally, Sophie Rogge. Back row (l-r): Lee Byrne, Peter Phillips, Daniel Dunne, Darragh Farrell, Louise McDermott.

depths in which to swim. Eddie O'Brien, team leader, said:

> Sea lions are social animals but at times they also like to get away from each other for a little while. The islands and caves allow them to do that. We monitor them during the night on cameras and they often sleep on one island together.

The streams running through the Sea Lion Cove flow on to the Flamingo Lagoon and the section of the lake where flamingos have been living since 1903. Until recent years, it had been necessary to pinion the birds to prevent them from flying away; this involved the amputation of part of a wing. However the decision had been made to stop pinioning birds in Dublin Zoo some years earlier; feather clipping was used until the construction of the great flight aviary in 2015 made even this temporary measure unnecessary. The results were soon seen. In 2018 the Chilean flamingo colony produced ten viable chicks, a record for Dublin Zoo. By not interfering with the wings, the matings were more balanced. The aviary protected the eggs and chicks from predators including seagulls, magpies, otters and foxes. With 98 birds in 2018, the Flamingo Lagoon colony became one of the largest in any zoo. The size of the colony gives the birds more partner choice and an increased sense of security.

Dublin Zoo's change of approach was timely; in 2014, campaigns in various countries had led to an announcement in the Netherlands that a total ban on pinioning birds would be introduced in that country from 2018 onwards. The Netherlands gave notice that it intended to lobby other EU countries to do the same.

Orangutan Forest

The 2016 project, the Orangutan Forest was inspired by the tropical rainforests of Borneo, the orangutans' natural environment, which Leo Oosterweghel had visited as a young man; he recalled:

> I was in a forest when I realised I was being watched from above and I stopped still. Looking up, I saw an orangutan observing

Flamingo at nest in
Flamingo Lagoon.

me. She stayed there for a while then carried on, moving along the upper branches of the trees. This is what I wanted visitors to Dublin Zoo to experience.

The idea of having orangutans crossing above the visitors' path became a core feature of the new habitat in Dublin Zoo. Design team member, Paul O'Donoghue, assistant to the director (animals and grounds), went to Washington DC to gather information at the National Zoological Park where orangutans had been crossing over a public path along a cable for 20 years without incident. Using a cable over the visitors' path in Dublin Zoo would not only create the possibility of a wonderful experience for visitors but it would also give the orangutans access to a newly-created meandering island in the lake and significantly increase the size of their habitat.

Nine artificial trees each between seven and 12 metres high were created, some in the transformed original habitat and some on the new island. Cables and ropes were hung from the trees and between tree tops to allow the animals to move around. Sturdy elevator shafts, designed in Ireland and orangutan-proof, were installed inside six of the trees. Operated by remote control, the small elevators take the food to the tops of the trees, giving the apes an incentive to climb and explore. The Siamang gibbon, native to the forests of south-east Asia, was introduced to the habitat and both species of ape settled well together.

Animal rights and especially rights for great apes took a leap forward in 2015 when an Argentinean court ruled that an orangutan is a 'non-human person'. Acutely aware of this, Operations Manager Gerry Creighton said: 'There were a lot of people questioning how we look after the animals, especially the apes. We need to be really conscious of what we are doing and how we are doing it.'

In Ireland, the Orangutan Forest became the focal point of a strong conservation message about how the orangutans' natural habitat in Borneo is rapidly shrinking, especially as a result of palm oil deforestation. In June 2016, when the Orangutan Forest was formally opened, a weekend of fundraising in Dublin Zoo and around the city raised nearly €19,000 for habitat protection. Rowan Sharp from the Orangutan Foundation, an *in situ* conservation project supported by Dublin Zoo, gave a talk to the whole Zoo team about their work in Kalimantan. Scientist Lorraine Bull was commissioned to write a report on the use of palm oil in the Zoo's restaurant and retail outlets in order to create a strategy to reduce its use. When team leader Ciaran McMahon and keeper Aisleen Greene travelled with Moondance to Kalimantan in Indonesia to visit the Orangutan Foundation in Pangkalan Bun, they experienced how the palm oil plantations were pushing the great apes into smaller and smaller spaces. Information about how to look out for palm oil in products and how to look for products that use palm oil from sustainable sources became part of the Dublin Zoo's message to visitors.

Sibu in the Orangutan Forest, which was opened in 2016.

Ruth Breen from Burnchurch National School, County Kilkenny, opening the Orangutan Forest in 2011, with (l-r) director Leo Oosterweghel (partly hidden), president of the Zoological Society of Ireland Tom Dunphy, and head of the Discovery and Learning Department Aileen Tennant. Ruth won a competition in which she wrote a poem that captured the magic of the new Orangutan Forest habitat.

View of the Orangutan Forest from across the lake.

Top: Sibu walking above the public path in the Orangutan Forest. **Below**: The West Side team at the opening of the Orangutan Forest. (l-r): James Creighton, Kelly Taponen, Thomas Munslow, Julie Bevins, team leader Ciaran McMahon, Alan Duffy, Aisleen Greene, Gerard Corbally.

Left: Gus Gallagher (left) and Michael McGowan using the interactive app on the Eco Explorer Trail in Dublin Zoo, 2019. This station at the Orangutan Forest encourages visitors to become more aware of palm oil in everyday products and encourages them to look out for products using palm oil from sustainable sources. **Right**: Una Smyth, Education Officer from 1999 to 2015, and assistant to the education officer, 1994–1999.

New sponsorship

By now Dublin Zoo had become a trusted source of information about conservation of animals and preservation of natural habitats and it was easier to present strong 'take-home' messages without compromising the relaxing family day out. In 2017 the Zoo announced a new five-year agreement with the power company SSE Airtricity. Unlike previous sponsorships, SSE Airtricity was not supporting a single habitat. Marketing manager, Emma Kiernan, explained:

> Sustainability is a core value at SSE Airtricity, as they are committed to providing the energy people need in a reliable and sustainable way. The partnership will help us to educate Dublin Zoo visitors, in a fun and interactive manner, about sustainability and the positive impact it has on the natural world and its wildlife.

SSE Airtricity created a bespoke 'Eco Explorer Sustainability Trail' in the Zoo with ten sustainability stations for parents and children to discover, enjoy and learn about how the Zoo uses recycled water and plastics, and what it does with dung. It also encourages children to create a bug hotel in their own gardens and to think about recycling everything from bottles to clothes and toys. All of these developments are communicated to the Zoo's audience of more than 380,000 people on Facebook, Twitter and Instagram.

Retail

In 2013 Emma Kiernan and retail manager Mark Bowes engaged retail consultant Sorintha Brady to undertake a thorough survey of the Dublin Zoo shops. Arising out of this, the gift shop was redesigned, the quality of items was improved and strong Dublin Zoo branding was introduced. Mark Bowes and the Retail team sourced new product lines from companies such as The Nature Planet, which is a Fairtrade company. A book corner and a new clothes range were introduced. Acutely aware of the important role retail plays in promoting the conservation message and environmental awareness, the team sources items that fit with the Zoo's philosophy such as reusable bamboo cups and biodegradable ponchos. All products including ice creams are either palm oil free or they use palm oil from sustainable sources. As time goes on, the retail team are sourcing more items made from recyclable materials or from sustainable sources. The result of these developments is evident in the quality of gifts now available in Dublin Zoo and the rising sales.

Discovery and learning

During all of these years of development, the Education Department and volunteers of Dublin Zoo had been working hard to communicate with visitors, each year adding to its impressive calendar of events and courses. And in 2017 and 2018, the time had come to fully implement the vision for education

Above: The Retail and Visitors' Services teams on a visit to Fota Wildlife Park during the visit of Pope Francis to the Phoenix Park in 2018. The Zoo's closure on 25, 26 and 27 August was exceptional and the only time the team could take a day away together. Back row (l-r): Frances Quinn, Patricia Kennerk, Pauline Marks, Florica Rascau, Doris Holland, Catherine Doggett, Mark Bowes (retail services and visitors' manager), Ann Costello, Gemma Kerrigan, Aoife Murphy Front row (l-r): Orla Lyons, Niamh Hanley, Noel Duffy, Leah Darcy, Kayleigh Cumiskey, Michelle Doyle, Emma Corrigan.

Primary schoolchildren arriving for a visit to Dublin Zoo, 2011.

with three new developments; Zoorassic World, Wild Space and the purpose-built Discovery and Learning Centre. Úna Smyth, who succeeded Michelle Griffin as education manager in 1999, had extended the Zoo's network with primary and secondary schools and developed programmes that were useful to hard-pressed teachers. In 2005, Dublin Zoo was accredited as a Discover Science Centre. And in 2008 the Department of Education and Science endorsed the Zoo's educational programmes, prompting increased demand for secondary courses and earning the praise of the Minister of Education, Mary Hanafin. These were major achievements for a small team still working with very modest resources.

In 2015 Úna Smyth retired and Aileen Tennant, a secondary school science teacher, was appointed head of the Discovery and Learning Department, renamed to reflect the extensive range of informal and formal programmes delivered with the help of volunteers. Several full-time and part-time teachers with

backgrounds in education and zoology were appointed, in-service training was stepped up, and links to schools, teachers and educators were further developed.

Zoorassic World

An important new educational facility was established with the opening in 2017 of Zoorassic World. It is located in the 1902 Roberts House, which was gutted and refurbished with help from conservation architects as well as Jones and Jones and the Zoo team. The glass roof was restored and the windows opened up, filling the old lion house with light. Zoorassic World was designed with extensive input from the Discovery and Learning team and the result is a clever combination of habitats for living reptiles and interpretative teaching facilities about extinct reptiles and related subjects.

At the heart of Zoorassic World was the intention to create a carefully planned learning space for visitors

Clockwise from top: Pat Kenny (centre), broadcaster and son of elephant keeper, Jimmy Kenny, opening Zoorassic World, July 2017. With director Leo Oosterweghel (left) and President of the Society Tom Dunphy; Cara and Brian Traynor, young descendants of keepers Thomas, Christopher and Charlie Flood, at the mural of a life-sized Diplodocus outside Zoorassic World; A replica of Charles Darwin's study at Down House, Kent, in Zoorassic World. It was created in the former lion-keepers office in the Roberts House.

Dublin Zoo teacher Kelly Mara with children in 'Dinosaur Discovery', a dig zone in Zoorassic World with specialist equipment and models of fossils designed to engage children in the work of a palaeontologist.

Alfie Conroy with 'Stan', a life-size replica fossil skeleton of an adult male Tyrannosaurus rex in Zoorassic World.

Teacher Kelly Mara with young student in the Wild Space.

of all ages. Aware of the latest changes in the school curricula, especially in the secondary level Junior Cycle, the Discovery and Learning team designed interpretation around courses well suited to teaching in Dublin Zoo. Two new programmes were launched at the Young Scientist & Technology Exhibition in 2018. Aileen Tennant said:

> We deliver a lot of science education in the Zoo. We are an incredible resource to schools across Ireland and have unique learning spaces to support teaching and learning. At the Young Scientist Exhibition, we meet teachers and students who are interested in science and the natural world so we can tell them what we can deliver. In 2018, we focused on two programmes, Evolution and Sustainability, which support the objectives of the national curriculum as well as the Zoo's own mission.

Wild Space

Wild Space, an immersive woodland classroom which opened in May 2018 in a secluded part of the African Plains, was the next notable development. Although

a small project, it drew together many strands of the Discovery and Learning Department's activities. The wild classroom was created for an innovative course, Families Connecting with Nature, a programme developed by Aileen Tennant and the Discovery and Learning team for delivery by the Zoo's teachers, external experts and volunteers. It was made possible by funding from the Disney Conservation Fund secured through the World Association of Zoos and Aquariums (WAZA) following a highly competitive process.

The funding, augmented by Dublin Zoo, was used to set up the infrastructure around Wild Space, and to design the course and prepare materials. Fourteen families from the local area were invited to attend the first programme in 2018, which took place one Saturday morning each month from April to August. Many of the families lived in high rise apartment blocks with little or no access to green spaces. Some had grown up abroad and were learning about Irish wildlife for the first time. With Zoo teacher Kelly Mara as the chief facilitator, the course drew on the extensive knowledge base amongst the volunteers as well as experts from Birdwatch Ireland, National Biodiversity Data Centre and the Office of Public Works. The participants were given packs including bird, butterfly and tree identification kits, and encouraged to spend time in Phoenix Park extending their new knowledge after the course.

The programme was a great success with a positive shift in attitudes towards the natural world on the part of the families over the five months. Dublin Zoo volunteer Ita Kelly said,

> The trainers and the group spent an extended period of time together, so everyone became very comfortable with each other. I remember one little girl who was afraid of everything at first but was soon leading the way looking for bugs! I also watched adults who had no confidence in their knowledge of nature coming to realise that they knew far more than they thought.

In 2018 the Discovery and Learning Department once more successfully applied through WAZA for funding from the Disney Conservation Fund to deliver the course again. With the infrastructure now in place and the course designed, the intention is to extend the programme to a greater number of families during the summer in 2019 and beyond.

Discovery and Learning Centre

The opening of the Discovery and Learning Centre in 2018 by President Michael D. Higgins was another milestone for education in Dublin Zoo. After 32 years of working from temporary bases around the Zoo, the Zoo's Discovery and Learning team at last had a substantial, purpose-built home with a museum, a large lecture theatre, classrooms, and staff and student amenities, all fitted out to a high standard. Also designed with appreciable input from the Discovery and Learning Department, the superb facilities provide immersive education experiences in biodiversity, conservation, ecology and zoology. The museum-quality biofacts, gathered throughout the years and augmented with many new items, are in the Discovery and Learning Centre where volunteers are stationed to help with enquiries. The interpretation is designed to

Zoo teacher Fiona McCann with secondary school students in the Discovery and Learning Centre.

Clockwise from top left: Discovery and Learning Centre, exterior; Alfie Conroy showing a Macleays spectre stick insect to President Michael D. Higgins and Mrs Sabina Higgins at the opening of the Discovery and Learning Centre, 2018; The Discovery and Learning team 2019 (l-r): Kelly Mara, Fiona McCann, Enya Cody, John Muldowney, Noreen Fitzsimons, Aileen Tennant and Christine O'Connor.

stimulate the curiosity of passing visitors. It also supports the formal environmental and conservation education programmes that are delivered to students by the team. The integrated thinking that went into the design, planning and construction of the new centre contributes significantly to Dublin Zoo's commitment to promoting animal conservation awareness and education.

Volunteers

The body of knowledgeable and skilled volunteers is central to the success of education in Dublin Zoo. By 2018 they were an integral part of the Zoo team but in the early 2000s the situation had been quite different. They had struggled with poor resourcing, and in spring 2001 had reached a crisis point. During the period in

Dublin Zoo volunteers gathered to celebrate the graduation of the 2019 programme. Front row (l-r) Patricia Pickett, Christel Sudway, Anne May, Mary Neville, Noreen Fitzsimons, Leo Oosterweghel, Aileen Tennant, Mary Timbs, Helen Curry, Rosemary Fulton, Annette Gavin. Second row (l-r) Eve Rochfort, Isolde Byrne, Birgit Berkenkopf, Melissa Hunter, Kathryn Murphy, Emily Gorman, Nori Krupp, Ríona Walsh, Maeve McDonald, Emma King, Catherine Gorman, Michelle Murphy. Third row (l-r) Lesley Penney, Eidin Finlay, Cáit Ní Chadhain, Val Goodwin, Aicha Aboudinar, Antoinette Nolan, Karen Feeney, Meadhbh O'Leary, Conor D'Arcy, Katja Jurasova, Clare McManus, Sarah Cox. Back row (l-r) Sarah Kennedy, Bridget Delaney, Aileen Rock, Daniel Dunleavy, Feidhlim Dockrell, Scott Murphy, Gimel Van der Linde, Judith Hayes, Sandra Fox, Shay Giles, Patricia Egan, Dean Notaro, Rebecca Murray, Briana Sheils, Iqbal Kanhiraparambil, Charlotte Molloy.

which Dublin Zoo was closed for nine weeks due to the foot-and-mouth crisis, a meeting was called in a nearby hotel by the volunteers to ascertain levels of interest within their own body. Long-term volunteer Maeve McDonald described the response:

> I thought people wouldn't be bothered coming. We were at our lowest point and if the interest wasn't there, we wanted to close it down and not just let it bleed to death. But there was a huge turnout and then I knew that we were going to be okay! Loads of people contributed to the discussion. It was very heartening.

A new volunteer coordinator was appointed and soon the communication system with rosters was functioning once more. Shortly afterwards, Leo Oosterweghel arrived as director. Coming from Melbourne Zoo, he was familiar with the role that a well-trained and enthusiastic body of volunteers can play in supporting a zoo; he also valued their knowledge and interest in the core objectives of the Zoo. The volunteers were organised into groups to utilise strength, experience and interest, and their uniform was streamlined to the now-familiar bright red tops.

In 2017 the volunteers celebrated 30 years of the programme and the Volunteer Centre opened with meeting spaces, offices and a workshop for their exclusive use. In 2018 the Discovery and Learning Centre became the home for their large collection of biofacts, the skulls, eggs, tortoise shells, horns and antlers and others, all prepared in such a manner that young visitors could touch them. The rigorous training course for new volunteers continues and each year up to 30 recruits graduate. Over the past ten years, the programme has doubled both in size and in the number of shifts delivered. There is a solid retention of volunteers who can commit to a roster all year round and in 2018, 113 people were available to help in the Zoo on a regular basis. Noreen Fitzsimons, appointed volunteer coordinator in 2009, said:

> There is great diversity in the backgrounds of our volunteers and they all share a common bond in their interest and love of animals and their dedication to the natural world and its conservation. I'd imagine that given the current climate the Dublin Zoo volunteer team feel part of a global movement and they have a commitment to the wider cause of spreading the word regarding conservation and the challenges that face vulnerable species in the world today.

From 2017, a specialist group of volunteers was recruited largely from teacher training colleges and university

Citron-crested cockatoo in Dublin Zoo.
Dublin Zoo registrar/research and
conservation coordinator, Sandra Molloy,
is European Endangered Species
Programme coordinator for the
critically endangered cockatoo.

zoology courses to support the ever-popular summer children's camps.

Informal education

The volunteers became crucial to the delivery of informal education in the Zoo as the number and variety of activities grew each year. The wealth of knowledge and teaching experience amongst the volunteers is harnessed to support many of the informal weekend workshops. They lead clubs such as bird watching, nature detectives and wild behaviours, and they design and deliver informal educational activities that appeal to visitors who are on a day out in the Zoo. In recent years, the focus of the programme has moved away from arts and crafts tables to being 'ambassadors for conservation' with a strong educational focus on their work. During their encounters with visitors, they deliver practical take-home messages for conservation awareness, such as looking at what they are buying, reusing specific items, observing birds, noticing trees, even watching the Zoo's animals online. In the Zoo they also deliver animal-themed events and many of their activities tie in to international animal events such as International Orangutan Day and World Elephant Day.

Conservation and research

The maturity of Dublin Zoo's role in biodiversity, animal conservation and environmental awareness by 2018 is not to be underestimated. When conservation and research were announced as two of the four objectives of modern zoos in the 1960s, there was little guidance as to what that meant in practical terms. Research had long been a role undertaken by major zoos but conservation as a coordinated objective was new. The most obvious task for zoos was to work cooperatively, breed endangered animals and maintain accurate studbooks. At the very least, should a species become extinct in the wild, there would still be animals with pure genes in zoos. At best, animals could be reintroduced to the wild but with natural habitats being eroded by the day and some species being reduced to mere hundreds of animals, zoos had to find other methods of contributing usefully. In 2005

Panther chameleon in Zoorassic World.

the World Association of Zoos and Aquariums (WAZA) drew these ideas together and issued the World Conservation Strategy that laid out a plan in which all of the operations of a zoo would work together to deliver a complex conservation message to its visitors. With 700 million people visiting WAZA zoos each year, the potential for influencing true change was consequential.

By this stage, Dublin Zoo was ready to work in harmony with this plan. In 2006 Sandra Molloy was appointed to the position of registrar/research and conservation coordinator with the additional responsibilities of coordinating conservation and research in Dublin Zoo. Molloy said:

> The vision for the Zoo was that we would be creating world-class habitats and linking them to what is happening in the wild. We would support *in situ* projects but we would be specific about who we supported. For example, we would have a habitat for western lowland gorillas in Dublin and we support the Mbeli Bai programme that works with the western lowland gorillas in the Democratic Republic of the Congo. Over time this would help our visitors to develop a clear picture of what we were doing in the Zoo and relate it to what was happening in the wild.

In 2006 Dublin Zoo was already financially supporting several *in situ* programmes, including the Golden Lion Tamarin Association in Brazil, West African Primate Conservation Action in Ghana and Birdwatch Ireland. Over the following years, the number of programmes supported by Dublin with regular sums of money and regular fundraising by the Zoo team increased; in 2018, Dublin Zoo supported 20 field projects, two international projects (Frozen Ark and Conservation Planning Specialist Group) and five native species projects as well as provided funding to the EAZA campaign, 'Silent forests: Asian songbird crisis'. Communication between Dublin Zoo and the *in situ* projects is constantly maintained through reports and emails, and occasionally by talks to the Dublin Zoo team by project workers visiting Europe. And of course the visits of Dublin Zoo keepers to several *in situ* projects in the company of a Moondance television crew strengthened the line of communication and introduced the *in situ* work to a large audience. These relationships have generated goodwill, supporting fundraising and allowing for useful knowledge exchanges between the keepers and the field workers.

Like many zoos, the Dublin Zoo team contributes to international, multi-zoo research projects. Dublin Zoo also undertakes research on animals they work with. Observation has always been important but with much larger habitats and demanding workloads, keepers find it challenging to make the time necessary to study in detail the animals they care for. Several keepers use their own time to watch the CCTV recordings of the animals and analyse whatever data they pick up during the routine part of their work. In some cases the work has been published; in 2012 a paper by keepers Louise McDermott and Peter Phillips on using the length of a flamingo's leg to predict the gender of a Chilean flamingo was published in the prestigious *International Zoo Yearbook*. And in 2017

Left: In 2011 a series of historical signs were erected to highlight the long history of Dublin Zoo. At the sign near the starting point for elephant rides in the mid-twentieth century are (l-r) Frank, Mary, Paul and Anne Marie Kenny, grandchildren and children of legendary elephant keepers James (keeper 1898–1940) and Jimmy Kenny (keeper 1933–1975).
Below: Scimitar horned oryx and calf in the African Savanna.

Images from Wild Lights, the spectacular night-time winter events held November 2017–January 2018, and November 2018–January 2019. Wild Lights was a marketing initiative to drive footfall to Dublin Zoo during the off-peak months. Giant colourful lanterns inspired by wildlife lit up the southern part of the Zoo after dark. The animals were in their night quarters. For visitors, the Meerkat Restaurant and refreshment stalls were open. Over 155,700 people visited in 2017–2018, and 210,235 in 2018–2019. In 2018 the Marketing Team won five industry awards for this event including the prestigious 'Best PR for an Event' at the Public Relations Consultants Association awards in 2018. Beth Healy (opposite page) with Nina Kiernan (top left) and Amelia Twomey (top right).

Leo Oosterweghel with a red-footed tortoise.

Zoological Society of Ireland council, senior staff and guest, 2018. Back row (l-r): Leo Oosterweghel (director), Neil O'Carroll (chairman of Fota Wildlife Park), Ann Keenan, Andy Beer, Carmel O'Connor, Paul Burke-Kennedy, John McMahon, John Sweeney (financial controller). Front row (l-r): Nigel Bell, Margaret Sinanan, Michael Daly (president), Tom Dunphy, Dorothy Kilroy. Missing: Jim McMonagle.

keeper Brendan Walsh's research on how elephants sleep, which he had conducted over several years, was published in the peer-reviewed *Journal of Zoo and Aquarium Research*.

The council and the future

In 2018 the council of the Zoological Society of Ireland approved a new master plan, *Dublin Zoo, 2018–2028 Physical Master Plan*. The complex plan incorporates ethics, conservation, sustainability, animal wellness, education and research, and builds on the achievements of the Zoo since the 2006 master plan. In it Leo Oosterweghel states:

> The time has come to look forward [and] set a new standard of care for animals, and establish a new vision and direction for future zoo leadership in wildlife conservation.

The council, the successors of the men who gave instructions on the diet of the wild boar or the accommodation for the bear 187 years earlier, continues to be the governing authority of Dublin Zoo. Its role shifted during the directorship of Peter Wilson as more zoo professionals were appointed to take over the operational duties formerly carried out by the council. In 2008 under the guidance of the president, Michael McNulty, the size of the council was reduced from a fluctuating number between 25 and 30, to 12 members, but all still voluntarily giving their time and expertise to maintain an overview of operations and provide support to the professional Zoo team.

Conclusion

In October 2018 the World Wildlife Fund reported that humanity had wiped out 60 per cent of the world's mammals, birds, fish and reptiles since 1970. Many in the zoo world were acutely aware of the ongoing threats to wildlife through human encroachment but the stark figure attracted headlines in mainstream media. Since the 1960s superb wildlife films, tourism to once-exotic destinations and safari encounters with animals in the wild were expected to make zoos obsolete but still the animals' wild habitats are being eroded through the activities of humans. The global zoo community recognised the threats early on and for nearly 60 years has been working to stem the destruction and conserve the most endangered species.

Dublin Zoo, like many other zoos, is striving to make a difference, to raise awareness and give hope and assistance to those visitors who want to do something. Of course it is still the animals that people come to see: the southern white rhinoceros, the Asian elephant, the Asian lion, the bongo, the white-naped mangabey, the western lowland gorillas, the meerkats, the red pandas. But every aspect of the Zoo's work, all of the efforts of the Zoo team, the selection of animals, the habitats, education, marketing, horticulture, retail and catering are aimed at encouraging visitors to participate in protecting and improving humans' relationship with animals and their natural environment.

In 1830 Philip Crampton, visionary founder of the Zoological Society of Ireland, hoped that visitors would develop a greater sensitivity towards wild animals by getting to know them in the Zoo. As Dublin Zoo approaches its bicentennial year, the words and intentions of Philip Crampton are still highly relevant. Back then there were lively discussions and debates about introducing laws to prevent cruelty to animals. Now humans threaten the extinction of species through encroachment on habitat, environmental damage and climate change. Dublin Zoo's role in generating sensitivity towards animals and their natural habitats is perhaps greater and more urgent than it was in the 1830s. Knowledge and awareness generated by contact with animals in a zoo can last a lifetime and contribute to a critical mass of concerned people who can make a difference.

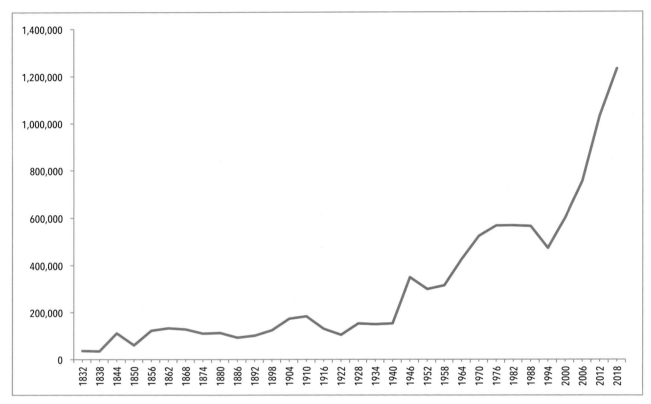

Visitor numbers from 1832 (36497 visitors) to 2018 (1,230,145 visitors).

The Dublin Zoo team, May 2019. Front row: (l-r) Suzanne O'Donovan, Aoibheann O'Flynn, Noel Duffy, Paul Kelly, Jimmy Prior, Anne Pennie, Susan O'Brien, Anne May, Mary Marsh, Patricia Pickett, Kelly Mara, Fiona McCann, Sandra Molloy, Enya Cody, Patricia Quinn, Val Goodwin, Aisling Kenneally, Sheila Denby, Karen Carrighy, Marie Kenny, Carmen Parfeni, Liliana Ursache, Irina Tamas, Iordache Halaida. **Second row: (l-r)** Lee Byrne, Kerri Conlon, Christina Murphy, Sean Mullan, Kelly Hamilton, Jason Murphy, Scott Murphy, Christine O'Connor, Bernadette Byrne, John Muldowney, Rebecca Murray, Kathryn Murphy, Noreen Fitzsimons, Louise McDermott, Aoife Murphy, Georgia Cooney, Gemma Kerrigan, Rose Capitano, Ken Mackey, Chris Fusco, Darragh Farrell, Pat Kane, Conor McMahon. **Third row: (l-r)** Aileen Tennant, Raymond Middleton, Niamh Hanley, Vlatka Jezernik, Paula Trifan, Mark Bowes, Stephen Kelly, Gerard Corbally, Anthony McClure, Gretchen Doyle, Ciaran Hogan, Jonathan Doyle, Adam Matthews, Getter Fernandez. **Back row: (l-r)** Raymond Mentzel, Mark Mooney, Gabriel Chirila, William Phillips, Laurentiu Axinte, Eoghan Gallagher, Declan Harmon, Amy Vickers, Jennifer Kenna, Leo Oosterweghel, Emma Kiernan, John Sweeney, Gerry Creighton, Ciaran McMahon, Angela Conroy.

Map of Dublin Zoo

1 Sulawesi crested macaque	20 Red-capped mangabey
2 Asian lion	21 Chimpanzee
3 Snow leopard	22 White-crowned mangabey
4 Citron-crested cockatoo	23 Painted dog
5 Bornean orangutan	24 Abyssinian ground-hornbill
6 Siamang gibbon	25 African spurred tortoise
7 Red-ruffed lemur	26 Red river hog
8 Ring-tailed lemur	27 Okapi
9 Grey wolf	28 Eastern Bongo
10 Amur tiger	29 Asian elephant and blackbuck
11 California sea lions	30 Red panda
12 Humboldt penguin	31 Chilean flamingo
13 Hippopotamus	32 Waldrapp ibis and white egret
14 Ostrich	33 Family Farm
15 Zebra	34 Brazilian tapir
16 Giraffe	35 Zoorasic World
17 Scimitar-horned oryx	(Reptiles Past and Present)
18 Southern white rhinoceros	36 South American House
19 Western lowland gorilla	37 Meerkat (viewed inside restaurant)

www.dublinzoo.ie

  **Do not feed the animals.
You will be asked to leave.**

Appendix 1

Presidents of the Zoological Society of Ireland, 1833–1837, and 1994 to date;
and the Royal Zoological Society of Ireland, 1838–1993.

Information taken from the president's chain of office and verified, where possible, from the annual reports.

1833	Sir Philip Crampton	1922–1926	Sir Robert H. Woods
1834	The Duke of Leinster	1927–1931	Professor A Francis Dixon
1835–1836	Captain Portlock R.E.	1932–1933	Sir William Taylor
1837–1838	Sir Philip Crampton	1934–1942	Lord Holmpatrick
1839–1840	The Archbishop of Dublin	1942–1943	Dr R. Lloyd Praeger
1841–1842	Sir Philip Crampton	1944–1950	Captain Alan S. Gordon
1843–1844	The Archbishop of Dublin	1951–1953	Professor John McGrath
1845–1846	Sir Philip Crampton	1954–1958	Dinnen B. Gilmore
1847–1848	The Duke of Leinster	1959–1961	George F. Mitchell
1849–1850	Sir Philip Crampton	1962–1964	N.Hamilton Lambert
1851–1852	The Marquis of Kildare	1965–1967	George Shackleton
1853–1854	Sir Philip Crampton	1968–1970	Professor Patrick N. Meenan
1855–1856	Lord Talbot de Malahide	1971–1973	Professor John Carroll
1857–1858	Sir Philip Crampton	1974–1976	Arthur E.J. Went
1859–1863	Dr D.J. Corrigan	1977–1980	Victor Craigie
1864–1869	Viscount Powerscourt	1981–1983	Alex G. Mason
1870–1871	Earl of Mayo	1984–1986	Aidan Brady
1872–1874	Earl Spencer	1987–1989	John D Cooke
1875–1878	Mr J. Murland	1990–1991	Padraig O'Nuallain
1879–1884	Sir John Lentaigne, C.B.	1992–1996	Professor David J.McConnell
1885–1889	The Rev. Dr Samuel Haughton, F.R.S.	1996–1999	Joe McCullough
1890–1892	Sir Robert Ball, F.R.S.	1999–2001	Sean Cromien
1893–1897	Dr Samuel Gordon	2001–2004	Michael O'Grady
1898–1902	Field Marshal Earl Roberts	2004–2005	Brian Murphy
1903	Professor D.J. Cunningham, F.R.S.	2005–2008	Michael McNulty
1904–1905	Earl of Dudley	2008–2011	Derek McCleane
1906–1910	Rt Hon. Jonathan Hogg, D.L., P.C.	2011–2014	Margaret Sinanan
1911–1915	Sir Charles Ball	2014–2017	Tom Dunphy
1916	Mr W.E. Peebles	2017–	Michael Daly
1917–1921	Sir Frederick Moore		

Appendix 2

Superintendents and directors of Dublin Zoo

Information is taken from the Zoological Society of Ireland minute books and full names have been listed where available. During the period when the minute books are missing, little precise information is available. In 1966 the title of the position was changed from 'superintendent' to 'director'.

c. July 1832	Francis Buckley
1833–1839	R. Drewitt
1839–1840	Mr Underwood
1840 to *c.* 1847	Mr Scott
c. 1847 to unknown date	Mr Buckley (possibly Francis Buckley)
Unknown date to 1862	James Henry Lowe
1862–1865	William Smith Batho
1865–1880	Edward Carter
1880–1890	Edward Sinclair Snow
1890–1891	Francis John Guy
1891–1907	Thomas Hunt
1907–1911	L. C. Arbuthnot
1911–1938	Benjamin Banks Ferrar
1938–February 1939	Acting superintendent Cedric Flood
February–March 1939	A. G. Doherty
March 1939–1952	Cedric Flood
1952–1956	Cecil Webb
1956–1984	Terry Murphy
1984–2001	Peter Wilson
2001 to date	Leo Oosterweghel

Endnotes

Most of the information in this book is taken from the minutes and annual reports of the Zoological Society of Ireland (ZSI) as it was known from 1830–1838 and from 1993 onwards, and of the Royal Zoological Society of Ireland (RZSI) as it was known from 1838–1993. Rough minutes only exist from May 1830 to July 1840 and from May 1860 to September 1865. No minutes are extant for the period August 1840 to April 1860. The minutes from 1830 to 1953 are in the Manuscripts Department of Trinity College Dublin.

Annual reports have been located for 1833, 1838, 1847, 1854–55, 1858 and from 1860 onwards. Records of the RZSI annual general meetings from 1840 to 1860 in the contemporary newspapers were compiled by the council in 1908 and published as *Proceedings of the society as reported in Saunders's News-Letter, the Dublin Evening Post and the Freeman's Journal.*

In the nineteenth century, unidentified newspaper cuttings were often inserted in the minute books; these are cited here by the date of the meeting to which they are attached. Letters from Robert Ball to the Zoological Society of London are held in its library.

For the new chapter covering the period 2000–2019, the ZSI council minutes continue to be the primary source of information. Newspaper articles, the quarterly magazine *Zoo Matters,* and eight series of the television programme *The Zoo* were also useful resources, especially with regard to individual animals, new habitats and the ongoing activities of the Zoo. The director's scrapbooks, which included articles from international newspapers and websites covering wide-ranging issues to do with zoos, wildlife and conservation, were a new resource for this history and were especially valuable in bringing a global perspective to the recent history of Dublin Zoo. Many staff members, including managers and team leaders, were interviewed for an up-to-date perspective on the work in their departments. Sources and dates of events have been embedded in the text in chapter seven where possible.

Chapter 1

1 Philip Crampton in *A report of the proceedings at a meeting held in the Rotunda, 10th May, 1830, to establish a Zoological Society.* Dublin, Joshua Porter, 1830.
2 *Ibid.* p. 26. The Cruelty to Animals Act outlawing this blood sport was passed in 1835.
3 ZSI rough minutes, 19 November 1832. For Drewitt's experience, reference ZSI rough minutes 30 August 1830 and for his appointment, 30 November 1832.
4 *Dublin Penny Journal*, December 1832, pp.181–182.
5 Information about Burton's plans is contained in a transcript of his report, dated 27 October 1832, in the ZSI rough minutes, 19 November 1832; drawings of the plans are not in the ZSI records.
6 In 1831 the population of the city of Dublin was 176,012; www.oldtowns.co.uk. The population was c.182,000 in 1800, and 258,369 in 1852, from Prunty, Jacinta, 'Improving the urban environment', in Brady, Joseph and Anngret Simms (Eds.)(2001), *Dublin through space and time*, Four Courts Press, Dublin, p.170.
7 Robert Ball to the Zoological Society of London, 23 December 1838, in the Zoological Society of London Library and Archives.
8 Robert Ball, 5 July, 1839, Zoological Society of London Library and Archives.
9 Memoir of James Haughton: with extracts from his private and published letters, by his son, Samuel Haughton; Longman, Green and company, Dublin, 1877, p. 46.
10 Report of the RZSI, in *Saunders' News-Letter*, Wednesday 5 May 1841.
11 ZSL minutes, 5 June 1844, 3 July 1844, and RZSI *Annual Report 1902*.
12 The minute books from this period of the Zoo are not extant and much of this information is gleaned from the daily transaction books, the annual report for 1847 and the extracts from *Saunders' News-Letter*.
13 RZSI *Annual Report 1854* p.6.

Chapter 2

1 Phillip Crampton donated the plesiosaurus fossil in 1853. It had been presented to him by the Marquess of Normanby. A special building, 12 metres long, was constructed for the exhibition of the delicate fossil. The fossil was deposited in the museum of the Royal Dublin Society in 1861. The fossil is now part of the collection of the National Museum of Ireland.
2 RZSI *Annual Report 1862–1863*, p. 14; RZSI *Annual Report 1863–1864*, pp. 16–17.
3 Information from *The Irish Times*, 17 Sept 1859; 14 August 1860; 20 May 1863.
4 RZSI visitors' notebook, late August, early September 1864.
5 RZSI visitors' notebook, 21 January 1865. RZSI *Annual Report 1867*, p.15. Edward Carter was a retired army lieutenant who had served in India; on his return to Ireland he had been governor of the Athy Jail and then a director of the Dublin Exhibition 1863 until it closed in 1865. Edward and

Maryanne had 15 children, three of whom were born while they lived in the Zoo. It was normal for the superintendent to look after sick animals at home and young family members helped out.

6   RZSI visitors' notebook undated entries around March 1865 and 6 June 1863. Also 29 December 1862, 4 January 1865, 8 December 1864 and 7 January 1865.

7   Details of the rhinoceros are in RZSI visitors' notebook various entries including 6, 30 and 31 August 1864, and 9 December 1864. Details of its illness and death are in RZSI visitors' notebook series of entries April 1865. RZSI rough minutes, 15 April 1865; report signed by Samuel Haughton.

8   Unidentified newspaper clipping in the minute book, 8 May 1869.

9   *The Irish Times*, 31 May 1870, p. 2. RZSI minutes, 26 August 1876 contain a reference to the fact that the omnibus company had ceased to run a bus to the Zoo. Population in Dublin city in 1881 was 249,602; Brady, Joseph, *Dublin through space and time*, Four Courts Press, 2001, p.262.

10 Unidentified newspaper article in RZSI minutes, 6 May 1871.

11 Unidentified newspaper article in RZSI minutes, 25 May 1872.

12 Unidentified newspaper article in RZSI minutes, 7 June 1873.

13 RZSI minutes, 13 September 1873.

14 Unidentified newspaper article in RZSI minutes, 11 January 1882.

15 *Brooklyn Daily Eagle* quote in unidentified Irish newspaper in RZSI minutes, 27 August 1870.

16 RZSI *Annual Report 1873*, p. 16. The rarity of the pygmy hippopotamus is such that Carl Hagenbeck, the famous animal dealer, is credited with the first successful capture and transportation to Europe of the smaller hippopotamus from Liberia in 1912 (Nigel Rothfels, 2002, *Savages and Beasts*, p. 219, Johns Hopkins University Press, Baltimore).

17 RZSI minutes, 22 August 1885.

18 Haughton's offer in RZSI minutes, 7 November 1889. Quote from anonymous council member in RZSI *Annual Report 1889*, p. 14.

19 Samuel Haughton's letter in the *Freeman's Journal and Daily Commercial Advertiser*, 10 March 1882, p. 5. Description of elephants' characters in unidentified newspaper article in RZSI minutes, 8 April 1882.

20 Unidentified newspaper article in newspaper clippings book, c.1883.

21 RZSI *Annual Report 1890*, pp. 15–17.

22 *Daily Express*, 31 July 1884, p. 6.

23 *Evening Telegraph*, 5 February 1891, p. 2.

24 *Daily Express*, 28 January 1891, p. 7.

25 *Freeman's Journal and Daily Commercial Advertiser*, 10 February 1891, p. 6.

26 *Evening Telegraph*, 5 February 1891, p. 2.

27 *Daily Independent*, 1 February 1893.

Chapter 3

1   Report containing recommendations for renovations and improvements inserted after the minutes of the RZSI meeting, 12 October 1895.

2   RZSI *Annual Report 1898*, pp. 19–20.

3   *The Irish Times*, 21 May 1902, p. 4 and p. 5.

4   *The Irish Times,* 21 May 1902, p. 4 and p. 5.

5   RZSI *Annual Report 1903*, pp. 5–6.

6   RZSI minutes, 13 February 1897. The official report of the accident on 16 May 1897 in the RZSI minutes, May 1897.

7   *The Irish Times*, 10 June 1903, p. 5; *The Irish Times*, 12 June 1903, p. 3; RZSI *Annual Report 1903* pp. 12–13. The record in the RZSI minutes on 13 June 1903 states that the incident happened on the evening of Wednesday 10 June 1903; however the report on the death is carried in *The Irish Times* on 10 June 1903.

8   RZSI *Annual Report 1914*. p. 7.

9   *Ibid.* p. 11.

10 *Freeman's Journal and Daily Commercial Advertiser*, 4 May 1915, p. 10.

11 The gorilla in the Breslau Zoologischer Garten, now the Wrocław Municipal Zoological Garden in Poland, lived from 1897 to 1904. *Encyclopedia of the World's Zoos*, Fitzroy Dearborn, 2001, p. 807.

12 RZSI minutes, 6 December 1919.

13 RZSI minutes, 6 March 1920. The periscope had been given to the Society by the Royal Navy War Trophies Committee in February 1920.

14 The Ladies' Committee was first established in 1903 to improve the quality of the refreshments in Haughton House. They ran the restaurant very successfully for three years and then announced their wish to pass the responsibility over to a manager (RZSI minutes, 7 July 1906).

15 Ferrar's advice concerning military transport, RZSI minutes, 3 January 1920. Postponing the dance, RZSI minutes, 6 November 1920.

16 RZSI minutes, 12 February 1921.

17 RZSI minutes, 25 March 1922.

Chapter 4

1   RZSI minutes, 9 June 1923.

2   *The Dublin Evening Mail*, 3 April 1923, p. 2. On 27 April, de Valera ordered the suspension of the Republican campaign and, in May 1923, the Republicans dumped their arms, thereby officially ending the Civil War.

3   The letter is in the RZSI minutes, 7 March 1925. All other references are taken from the lists of donations and the list of corresponding members in the annual reports.

4   *The Irish Times*, 28 February 1924, p. 5.

5   RZSI minutes, 13, 20, and 27 April, 11 May and 8 June 1940. Letter to *The Irish Times*, 25 April, 1940, p, 9. *Evening Mail*, 30 April 1940. Unidentified newspaper article dated 4 April 1940 in the Dublin Zoo archive. *The Irish Times*, 26 July 1940, p. 4.

6   RZSI minutes,3, 17 and 31 December 1938; RZSI minutes, 2 March 1940.

7   *Belfast Telegraph*, 8 September 1942; RZSI minutes, October 1945.

8   RZSI minutes, 13 September 1941.

9   RZSI *Annual Report 1940*, p. 5; RZSI minutes, 12 June 1943. Michael Ward, in conversation with the author in 2009, believed that it was his mother, Yvonne Ward's idea to create the Children's Corner.

10   RZSI minutes, 20 July 1940 and 22 February 1941.

11   RZSI *Annual Report 1941*, p. 4.

12   Michael Ward in conversation with the author in 2009.

13   *Evening Herald*, 16 February 1942.

14   *The Irish Times*, 6 September 1941.

15   *Sunday Independent*, 30 June 1946.

16   RZSI minutes, 6 December 1947 and *Annual Report 1947*, p. 6.

17   RZSI minutes, 6 July 1948 and 29 January 1949.

18   *Evening Mail*, 29 January 1949; *Irish Press* in July 1948; RZSI *Annual Report 1949*, p. 4.

19   RZSI minutes, 25 March 1944.

20   *Carlow Nationalist*, 1 July 1946.

21   'Visits to Dublin Zoo during the Second World War: transcribed from notes and diaries written at the time,' an unpublished paper by Seán Cromien, member of council from 1994 and president of the Society from 1999 to 2001.

22   RZSI minutes, 23 July 1949.

23   Report on this exchange was in *The Irish Times*, 8 December 1949, p. 1. When the Society's patron, King George V had died in 1936, the council had sent a message of condolence via the Department of External Affairs. A blank space remained under the heading 'patron' in the annual report until 1943.

Chapter 5

1   Murphy, Terry, *Some of my best friends are animals*, Paddington Press, 1979, pp. 129–130.

2   RZSI minutes, 2 February 1952, 1 March 1952 and 6 December 1952.

3   Gerry Creighton (junior) in conversation with the author, 2009.

4   The RZSI minutes, 9 September 1944 record that Terry Murphy's three-month probation period was completed. *Annual Report 1956* for information about the trip to the continent. *Official guide to the Dublin Zoo*, by Edward Terence Murphy, Royal Zoological Society of Ireland, undated but published in 1952 or 1953.

5   Tom McGrath, electrician and general maintenance man, in conversation with the author, 2008.

6   Retired keeper, the late Michael Clarke, in conversation with the author, 2009.

7   RZSI minutes, 29 March 1952.

8   Visitors in conversations with the author in 2008–2009, including Olwyn Lanigan, Ann Murphy, Dorothy Kilroy and Paul Kenny, and in 2019, Ann Stevens.

9   RZSI minutes, 5 July 1958; RZSI minutes, 17 January 1959.

10   RZSI *Annual Report 1950*, p. 8; RZSI minutes, 1 and 8 July 1950; Olwyn Lanigan in conversation with the author, 2009.

11   Terry Murphy, *Some of my best friends are animals*, p. 153.

12   Tony Tormey in conversation with the author, 2009.

13   Pam McDonough in conversation with the author, 2009; statistics from RZSI *Annual Report 1965*, p. 16; RZSI *Annual Report 1970*, p. 14.

Chapter 6

1   *Evening Herald*, 23 December 1982.

2   'Table for two', *The Irish Times*, 16 March 1985, p. 12.

3   Mary Glennon in the *Evening Herald*, 9 July 1985.

4   Information from *The Irish Times*, 20 February 1982; RZSI minutes, 20 February, 6 March, 17 April, 17 July 1982, and RZSI *Annual Report 1982* (p. 7).

5   Gerry Creighton (senior) in conversation with the author 2008. Abbotstown was the location of the Veterinary Research Laboratory, Department of Agriculture and Fisheries, where post mortems were carried out.

6   Dublin Zoo horticulturalist Stephen Butler in conversation with the author, 2008–2009.

7   RZSI *Annual Report 1983*, p. 19; minutes of the AGM 24 January 1981, in RZSI *Annual Report 1980*, p. 2.

8   *The Irish Times*, 9 May 1983, p. 1.

9   *The Irish Times*, 16 May 1983, p. 11.

10   *Irish Independent*, 4 October 1983. Concerning the strike, RZSI minutes, 15 October 1983.

11   *Sunday Independent*, 4 November 1984.

12   Peter Wilson in conversation with the author, 2009. RZSI annual reports, 1972, 1973, 1974 and 1984.

13   *Encyclopedia of the World's Zoos*, pp. 952–953.

14   Helen Clarke in conversation with the author, 2009. RZSI minutes, July 1987 contain a reference to a 'recent' accident; no date is given for the accident.

15   Dr Bill Jordan, wildlife expert; comparisons were made with the polar bear facilities in Bristol Zoo. The *Today Tonight* programme was broadcast on 14 March 1989.

16   RZSI minutes, 9 December 1989. Information concerning breakfast from council member and past president Michael O'Grady, in conversation with the author, 2009. Quote from RZSI minutes, 24 October 1989. On Haughey's response, *The Irish Times*, 26 February 1990.

17   Bertie Ahern in conversation with the author, 2009.

18   Dan Mahony in conversation with the author, 2009.

19   Dan Mahony in conversation with the author, 2009. RZSI minutes, October 1988; the bat house has since been demolished to make way for the Kaziranga Forest Trail.

20   *Report of the government-appointed committee to advise on Dublin Zoo*, Dublin Stationery Office, July 1990, pp. 49–50. It is known as 'The Doyle Report'.

21   ZSI minutes, 6 November 1993. *The Irish Times*, 22 June 1994, p. 11.

22   Stephen Butler, Martin Heffernan, in conversation with the author in 2008–2009.

23   Stephen Butler in conversation with the author in 2008–2009.

24   Úna Smyth in conversation with the author in 2009. Úna Smyth succeeded Michelle Griffin as education officer in January 1999. Fiona Gartland's article in unidentified newspaper from around September 2003 in the Dublin Zoo archive.

25   Bertie Ahern, T.D., in conversation with the author, 2009; Michael O'Grady in conversation with the author 2009; Dublin Zoo *Annual Report 1997*, p. 4.

Chapter 7

1   Dublin Zoo *Annual Report 2002*, p. 7.

2   Speech by Taoiseach, Mr Bertie Ahern, T.D., at the launch of *A Vision for Dublin Zoo*, in Dublin Zoo on Monday 25 September 2006.

3   *Zoo Matters* winter 2008, p.6.

4   *The Irish Times* online edition 5 June 2011.

Young African painted dog, born in Dublin Zoo in 2016.

Picture Credits

Many of the older images used in the book are from the Dublin Zoo archive, which includes substantial collections of glass slides and prints. Few of the photographers are identified on the casing of the slides or on the prints and, where they have been identified, every effort has been made to contact all copyright holders. The author would be happy to hear from any copyright holder not acknowledged and undertakes to rectify any omissions or errors in future editions.

Information used in the captions was taken, in most cases, from the casing of the glass slide or the back of the print, or from the lender. Animals in the pictures in chapters 5–7 have been identified with the help of current and former staff members.

Pp ii, vi, viii, xi, 50, 126 (upper), 128, 133, 135, 138, 140 (upper left), 141, 142, 143, 144, 145, 147 (upper and lower), 148, 149 (upper and lower), 150, 151, 152 (upper), 154, 155, 156, 157, 159, 160 (upper and lower), 161 (upper and lower), 162 (right), 163 (lower), 164 (upper and lower left), 165 (upper and lower), 166, 167, 168 (all), 171, 172 (left and right), 173 (lower), 174, 175 (all), 177, 179, 184 photos by Patrick Bolger; pp. 2 (left), 24, 25, 34 (lower left), 37 (upper), 38 (lower left), 40, 44, 48 courtesy of the Royal College of Surgeons in Ireland; pp. 2 (right), 12 (lower), 14, 22, 26, 30 (lower), 32, 33,35 (upper), 52 (lower left and right), 53, 54 (upper), 56 (centre and bottom), 57 images courtesy of the National Library of Ireland; pp. 4 (top), 16 (top left), 21 (lower), 47, 112, 132 (upper), 140 (lower right), 158, 162 (left), 164 (lower right), 173 (upper) photos by Damien Maddock; pp. 6 (lower left), 9 (top), 16 (top right), 20 (lower), 21 (upper) 42 courtesy of The Board of Trinity College Dublin; p. 17 courtesy of Grellan D. Rourke; p. 19 Getty Images; pp. 56 (top right), 59, 92 (upper) courtesy of Rowland Eustace; pp. 56 (top left), 58 (right), 67 (lower), 90 (lower right), 91 (left) courtesy of Paul Kenny; p. 60 (top right) courtesy of Hannah Dowling; p 63 (all photos) courtesy of Sarah Pyle; p. 64 (lower) courtesy of Alex Ward; p. 68 (all) courtesy of Elizabeth Moore; pp. 76 (top), 87 (lower) courtesy of Fiona Barrett; p. 76 (centre left) photo by Bill St Leger, courtesy of Joe St Leger; pp. 77, 79 photos by Douglas Duggan; p. 78 courtesy of Suzanne Montgomery Duggan; p. 80 courtesy of the O'Flynn family; p. 81 (left) courtesy of Libby McElroy; p. 81 (right) courtesy of Laura Grehan; pp. 82 (top left), 103 courtesy of Gerry Creighton (snr); p. 82 (top right) courtesy of Anthony Byrne; p. 82 (centre) courtesy of Mark Crowther; p. 82 (lower left) courtesy of Dorothy Kilroy; p. 82 (lower right), 94 (lower), 106 (upper) courtesy of The Irish Times; p. 85 (top left), 94 (upper) courtesy of The Irish Independent; p. 85 (top right) courtesy of David Coleman, Bobby Studio; p. 85 (bottom left) courtesy of Noreen Kenny; p. 85 (bottom right) courtesy of Alan Eaton; p. 90 (upper left) courtesy of Patty de Courcey; p. 90 (upper right) courtesy of Veronica McCormack; p. 90 (lower left), 114 (upper) courtesy of Maeve McDonald; p. 90 (lower centre) courtesy of Ann Stevens; p. 91 (right) courtesy of Liam Reid; p. 92 (lower) courtesy of Alison Breen; p. 95 (upper) courtesy of Pam McDonough; p. 96 (upper) courtesy of Majella Fergus; p. 96 (lower) courtesy of Kevin Breen; p. 104 photograph by Pat Sweeney; pp. 105 (upper and lower left), 107 (lower), 111, 114 (lower) courtesy of Elizabeth Sides; p. 107 (upper) photo by Jonathan Pratschke; p. 108 (upper) Fota Wildlife Park collection; pp. 109 (photo by Bob Hoby), 110 (photo by Ann Egan), 118, 119 (photos by Tony Gavin) courtesy of the Sunday Tribune; p. 121 courtesy of Fennell Photography; p. 122 courtesy of Mark Hogan; pp. 123, 131 courtesy of Neil McShane; p. 130 photo by Robbie Reynolds; p. 136 (lower left) courtesy of Grace Hefferon; p. 140 (lower left) courtesy of Rowland Reece; p. 152 (lower) courtesy of Ken Mackey; p. 163 (upper) courtesy of Orla Lyons.

Index